NEW
AMERICAN
CHEFS

AND THEIR RECIPES

OTHER BOOKS BY LOU SEIBERT PAPPAS

Entertaining in the Light Style
International Fish Cookery
The Elegant, Economical Egg Cookbook
Greek Cooking
Crockery Pot
Cookies
Creative Soups and Salads
Bread Baking
Gourmet Cooking—the Slim Way
Entertaining the Slim Way
Vegetable Cookery

NEW AMERICAN CHEFS

AND THEIR RECIPES

LOU SEIBERT PAPPAS
Preface by M.F.K. Fisher

101 PRODUCTIONS
SAN FRANCISCO

COLOR PHOTOGRAPHS (Including Cover): Renee Lynn (© 1984)

COVER AND TEXT DESIGN: Lynne O'Neil

BLACK AND WHITE PHOTOGRAPHS: Waring Abbott, p. 108 (© 1983);
Wallace Ackerman Studio, p. 118; J. Lewis Allen, p. 84; Trent Anderson, p. 75
(© 1983); D. Barnes, p. 21; California Photo, p. 16; Drake Photography, p. 71 (© 1983);
Faith Echtermeyer, p. 12; Richard Faughn, 43; Paul Glines, p. 51; Curt Granthen, p. 89;
Bill Jones, p. 122; Bryan Leatart, p. 36; Renee Lynn, *Peninsula Times Tribune*, pp. 67, 69;
Barbara Elliott Martin, p. 113; Bernard Mendoza, p. 7, Doug Mindell, p. 62 (© 1983);
Barbara Mortensen, p. 133; Richard Stack, p. 78; Brian Stanton, p. 40; Robie Ray, p. 137;
Carolyn Turner, p. 103; Michael Weiss, p. 98; Ken Yimm, *Peninsula Times Tribune*, pp. 25,
27, 56, 60, 141, 142.

Some of the text and recipes in this book are based upon articles by Lou Seibert Pappas,
originally published in the *Peninsula Times Tribune*, Palo Alto, California.

Printed and bound in the United States of America.

Distributed to the book trade in the United States
by The Scribner Book Companies, New York.

Published by 101 Productions
834 Mission Street
San Francisco, California 94103

Library of Congress Catalog Card Number   84-042847
ISBN 89286-240-8 Hardcover
ISBN 89286-239-4 Paperback

CONTENTS

PREFACE

Perhaps this book about a young, fresh look at our ways of public enjoyment of the art of eating in America is an unwitting proof that we are all Peeping Toms!

What Lou Pappas tells us with seeming artlessness about the people who cook and own some of our best and most exciting restaurants makes us read the recipes they have sent to her as if we were gastronomical *voyeurs*. We learn where they came from, and even how they decided to be cooks instead of doctors or artists or nuclear physicists. Then we read her own generous hints of why they are good chefs instead of poor or piddling or plain bad ones (Who ever said that cooks hide their best tricks, and never betray the Secret Ingredient? Some two hundred recipes sent freely and even joyfully prove that old saw false . . .), and we snoop happily for *clues*. We feel as if we had a free codebook to their mysteries.

And as we enjoy the freshness of their skillful use of fruits and vegetables and even flowers that we had almost forgotten about during our long, enjoyable years of servitude to classical cooking, we realize that these new young chefs are not naive kids splashing around happily in a freak success. They are very serious, dedicated people, studying and training and practicing for a completely fresh way of leading us from trough to table.

All good cooks have always tried to, of course. They have used their skills and wits to make us feel intelligent, sensitive, well-fed creatures instead of hungry animals. Sometimes they have had to bow to the so-called progress of history, as when enjoyment turned to satiety in Greek and Roman and finally European cultures. Perhaps we, too, were in danger of this subtle takeover of gluttony in the last few centuries. In their cartoons Rowlandson in London and Daumier in France were not always flattering to the predominance of Pig over Puritan in our fairly recent public lives . . .

Of course this new wave of interest in food that is fresh and seasonal and local is far from original. But probably never before have whole parts of our planet's nations been as aware as we are now of the pleasures of looking at a plate of food deliberately planned to be attractive as well as delicious, and still be able to believe that it will nourish the whole person in us, the hidden hungry animal.

There are many of us who cannot but feel dismal about the future of various cultures. Often it is hard not to agree that we are becoming culinary nitwits, dependent upon fast foods and mass kitchens and mega-vitamins for our basically rotten nourishment. But one or two grudging peeks at what the bright, brave young cooks say, and at the patterns they have evolved and toss proudly and gaily out to us in books like this one, will do much to soothe our spirits. We will, I know for a fact, feel a new encouragement. We will arise from our next meal not so much "resigned," like the poet, as refreshed, and ready to head for further pleasure at both the table and . . . even *elsewhere*.

M.F.K. FISHER
Glen Ellen, California
1984.

IN DEDICATION

Many thanks to a group of dedicated friends, the "sous chefs" who participated in weekend cooking feasts to turn out a spread of eighteen to twenty dishes nightly, thus testing the recipes for this book. A toast to Kirby Bennett, Carol and Earl Calkins, Dawn deCastro, Tina and Walter Dreyer, Mary Fortney, Edna Frescura, Jack Graf, Peter Hertzmann, William Johnson, Mary McGee, Trish and Roger Morf, Judy and Robert Peterson, Pradeep Rao and Virginia and James Tedrow. Many thanks, also, to a superb editor, Jane Horn.

INTRODUCTION

American restaurant cuisine has come of age. Call it a revolution or revelation, its expression is a return to freshness and simplicity in dining.

The movement has been quietly gaining momentum over the past decade or more, led by a new breed of innovative, talented, highly educated and dedicated chefs. Working with the freshest of ingredients in creative regional and ethnic styles, this coterie of young men and women has developed an exhilarating new cuisine, eclectic and personal.

Their repertoire is a showcase for seasonal bounty. Unusual combinations transform familiar fare. With a succulent filling of sweetbreads and wild mushrooms, unassuming, everyday ravioli achieves elegance. Subtle, sweet, grilled salmon quietly partners a lively chili pepper sauce. All-American apple and fragrant basil pair in a palate-cleansing sorbet.

Like its people, the style of this new American cuisine is a composite of many cultures. Its basis may be classic French, but when exposed to the heat of Latin American, Asian and Caribbean flavors, the result is lively, exciting, altogether original. America's own culinary heritage is now a respected resource. Today's chefs intertwine the exotic with favorites from their grandmothers' kitchens.

Previously scarce, seasonal and regional ingredients are now potentially within reach of any American chef because of improved methods of storage and transportation. The chefs delight in their expanded pantry.

A wealth of cottage industries has launched an abundance of new products and fresh ingredients including California goat cheese, Napa Valley virgin olive oil, berry and varietal wine vinegars, fresh herbs, chutneys and mustards, farmhouse cheddar, foie gras, golden caviar and freshwater crayfish.

American chefs are reveling in the rediscovery of native foods. Once extinct crops are again under cultivation. Prized indigenous foods include Olympia oysters, quail, pheasant, chukkar, venison, boar, buffalo, mussels, morels, wild huckleberries, beach plums, prickly pears, chayotes, maple syrup, wild rice, cranberries and blue corn.

Responding to demand, farmers are cultivating unglamorous oldtimers such as sunchokes, spaghetti squash and rutabagas and the more recently familiar cherimoyas, star fruit and radicchio.

Purveyors make available specialty foods from other countries. Such imports as Swedish reindeer, Norwegian salmon, New Zealand scallops and mussels, Thai spices and Chilean grapes appear with increasing frequency on restaurant menus.

The chefs included here present a mixed profile. What is unique about this generation is their youth (their average age is early thirties); their intellectual achievements (ninety-five percent are college graduates); and their dedication to an enjoyment of fine wine and food and the pleasures of the table.

Some entered culinary trade schools immediately after high school. Many left promising careers in publishing, public relations, the law and industry to wield a chef's knife. Still others chose not to pursue advanced degrees in such diverse fields as anthropology, psychology, physics and the arts to instead train on-the-job in professional kitchens.

Women have gained a long-deserved niche in the highly competitive culinary field. Perseverance, great stamina and ability have opened the door for them to a previously male-dominated domain. Among this group, more than one-fourth are women.

Throughout this country, many chefs and their restaurants are achieving superstar status, much like their multi-starred counterparts in France. It is time to showcase the talents of these promising culinarians. Here thirty-four chefs from across the nation share seasonal menus representative of their own establishments. Each dinner includes recipes for a first course, entrée and dessert, and, in some cases, suggestions for salad and vegetable accompaniments.

All of the chefs echo a common theme: freshness is the most important criterion. In tandem, lightness and clarity let true flavors emerge.

Hallmarks of their style are mesquite-grilled meats and fish; cured or smoked seafood; fresh pastas; freshly churned fruit sorbets and custardy ice creams; flourless chocolate cakes and an abundance of anything chocolate. Fresh herbs and spices are integral accents.

With enthusiasm they volunteered this collection of approximately two hundred recipes.

The recipes arrived for testing in all styles: neatly typed, in longhand on legal paper, dictated by telephone. Some were accompanied by fine pen and ink drawings showing the assembly of the dishes. Others were illustrated with color sketches detailing presentation. Together they present an intriguing portrait of today's top restaurants. The collection captures a moment in time in the professional lives of the contributing chefs. In the pursuit of new ideas and experiences, any or all of this very mobile group of men and women might be somewhere else tomorrow.

Whatever states the new chefs hail from, whatever regional cooking styles they embrace, they project an energy that is revitalizing dining out in America. One chef expresses the philosophy of many: "Food should be fun, full of life and gusto." For the men and women whose creations appear here, it is a philosophy aptly formulated and consistently applied.

NEW
AMERICAN
CHEFS

AND THEIR RECIPES

Leslie Revsin
BRIDGE CAFE
New York City, New York

After graduating from college with honors and a degree in painting, Leslie Revsin, 39, now chef of the Bridge Cafe in New York, experienced a sudden, dramatic urge to shift careers. "It was like a rocket going off inside me," explains Revsin, "when I realized I had to switch my career to food. Something took over and there is this passion that doesn't diminish."

Revsin entered New York Technical College for professional training. She then became "kitchen man" and subsequently the first woman chef at the Waldorf-Astoria hotel. She went on to work at many Manhattan restaurants and for four years had her own acclaimed nine-table Restaurant Leslie in Greenwich Village.

Her approach to food is artistic, intellectual and personal. With consummate skill she mixes unexpected tastes and textures in subtle combinations, but rejects trendiness and despises nouvelle cuisine. Her style is eclectic ("the best ingredients from everywhere") and honest. Her food tastes of what it is; what accompanies, supports. "It is simple and classic at the same time," she says.

Revsin expresses her philosophy toward food this way: "I cook for the deep pleasure—the sensuousness—of the task. Each ingredient has a special message to a chef and each chef responds differently. The result is a way of speaking to the customer."

The Bridge Cafe occupies one of the oldest buildings in New York City. Built in 1801 as a seamen's bar and hotel, the structure sits almost directly beneath the foot of the Manhattan end of the Brooklyn Bridge. It predates the span by more than three-quarters of a century. The dining room features the original bar, a stamped tin ceiling, red checkered tablecloths and small neon replicas of the Brooklyn Bridge in the windows. Flower-filled terracotta pots on the sills complete the mood, a mix of New York old and new.

Open for lunch weekdays, dinner nightly and weekend brunch, the restaurant offers such specialties as escargot with garlic butter and sun-dried tomatoes, fried quail with roasted peppers, fried sea scallops with red pepper salsa, pan-fried brook trout with bacon and grated lemon, roast chicken with ginger sesame butter, strawberry rhubarb pie, fudge cake and pecan tart.

A SPRING DINNER

Sea Scallops with Cabbage, Shallots and Cranberries

Mixed Green Salad with Shallot Vinaigrette

Tangerine Sherbet

SEA SCALLOPS WITH CABBAGE, SHALLOTS AND CRANBERRIES

2 teaspoons pork, duck or chicken fat, rendered, or olive oil
16 peeled whole shallots
5 tablespoons butter
4 cups shredded Savoy cabbage, lightly packed
¾ cup dry white wine
3 cups white Fish Stock (page 147)
⅓ cup sauterne
1 sprig fresh rosemary or ¼ teaspoon dried rosemary
Scant ½ cup fresh or frozen cranberries (thawed, if frozen)
Salt and freshly ground black pepper to taste
1 ½ pounds sea scallops, well-washed and patted dry
Fresh rosemary or parsley sprigs for garnish

In a large saucepan melt fat or heat oil. Add whole shallots and lightly brown. Add 2 tablespoons butter and the shredded cabbage. Cook over low heat until cabbage is wilted, stirring frequently. Add ¼ cup of the white wine, 1 cup of the fish stock, sauterne and rosemary. Cover and cook over very low heat for 30 minutes. Add cranberries and cook 5 minutes longer or until cranberries are just tender. Season with salt and pepper. Keep warm.

Season scallops lightly with salt and pepper. In a large skillet cook scallops in remaining 3 tablespoons butter about 2 to 3 minutes until browned but slightly underdone in the center. Remove scallops and keep warm. Deglaze pan with remaining ½ cup white wine. Boil rapidly to reduce sauce by half. Add remaining 2 cups fish stock and boil rapidly again to reduce stock to about ⅔ cup. Season with salt and pepper. To serve, arrange a spoonful of cabbage in the center of a plate and place sea scallops on two sides. Spoon the fish sauce around the scallops and garnish with fresh rosemary or parsley sprigs. Makes 4 servings.

MIXED GREEN SALAD WITH SHALLOT VINAIGRETTE

2 to 3 shallots
¼ teaspoon cracked black
  peppercorns
1 garlic clove, crushed
¼ cup balsamic vinegar
¾ cup extra virgin full-flavored
  olive oil
Salt to taste
3 heads assorted mixed greens,
  washed and crisped

Peel and chop shallots by hand (should have a scant ¼ cup). Place chopped shallots in a bowl with peppercorns, garlic and vinegar. Gradually whisk in olive oil to lightly emulsify. Add salt to taste. Place greens in a bowl and lightly mix with enough dressing just to coat. Makes 4 servings.

TANGERINE SHERBET

Sugar Syrup (following)
3 cups tangerine juice (about 10
  medium tangerines)
2 tablespoons fresh lemon juice

Prepare Sugar Syrup. For sherbet, combine tangerine juice with 9 tablespoons of cold, strained Sugar Syrup and lemon juice. Churn in an ice cream freezer following manufacturer's instructions until frozen. Makes about 1 ¼ quarts.

SUGAR SYRUP In a saucepan combine ¾ cup sugar and ¾ cup water. Bring to a boil over high heat and stir until sugar dissolves. Add the peel from 4 tangerines (the zest removed with a vegetable peeler) and bring the syrup to a full boil. Remove from heat immediately. Let cool, strain and refrigerate.

A WINTER DINNER

Sautéed Belgian Endive
with Caramelized Lemon

Filet Mignon
with Scottish Salmon,
Morels and Vintage Port

Red Swiss Chard
and Spinach Sauté

Espresso Crème Caramel

SAUTEED BELGIAN ENDIVE WITH CARAMELIZED LEMON

4 Belgian endives
Water
1 cup Chicken Stock (page 147)
2 tablespoons lemon juice
1 bay leaf
1 sprig fresh thyme or ¼
  teaspoon dried thyme
2 tablespoons fresh white
  bread crumbs, sautéed in 1
  tablespoon butter until golden
7 tablespoons unsalted butter
Salt and freshly ground black
  pepper to taste
1 strip thick-sliced smoked
  bacon, cut in ½ -by-1-inch
  pieces and cooked until crisp
Caramelized Lemon
  (following)

In a shallow pan arrange endive in 1 layer. Add 1 cup water, chicken stock, lemon juice, bay leaf and thyme. Cover and simmer very slowly until tender, about 30 to 40 minutes. Strain liquid. Boil rapidly to reduce to about 1 cup. Set aside. Cut endive in half lengthwise and set aside.

Heat 3 tablespoons butter in a sauté pan over medium heat until butter starts to turn light brown. Add the drained endive; season with salt and pepper and brown the endive on both sides. Place on plates in a warm oven. Pour off butter. Add braising juices to the sauté pan, bring to a boil and whisk in 4 tablespoons of cold butter, one tablespoon at a time, until the juices are slightly thickened. Season. Divide over endive. Sprinkle the toasted bread crumbs and bacon over each and top with a lemon slice. Makes 4 servings.

CARAMELIZED LEMON Combine ½ cup water and 2 tablespoons sugar. Place over low heat. When mixture just begins to caramelize, add 4 thin slices lemon. Turn the slices in the caramelizing liquid several times and continue cooking slowly for several more minutes or until the juices become a light brown. Set slices aside.

FILET MIGNON WITH SCOTTISH SALMON, MORELS AND VINTAGE PORT

1 ounce dried morel
  mushrooms, soaked in 1 ½
  cups warm water for several
  hours (liquid reserved)
⅓ cup sliced unpeeled shallots
3 ½ tablespoons butter
1 garlic clove, crushed
1 cup full-bodied dry red wine
Sprig tarragon or ¼ teaspoon
  dried tarragon
Sprig thyme or ¼ teaspoon
  dried thyme
1 bay leaf
4 cups strong brown Beef or
  Veal Stock (page 147)
¼ cup vintage port
4 filet mignons (6 to 7 ounces
  each)
Salt and freshly ground black
  pepper to taste
1 ½ teaspoons vegetable oil
4 tablespoons cold butter, cut
  in pieces
2 thick slices Scottish salmon,
  cut in ⅛ -by-1-inch strips

Drain mushrooms, reserving 1 cup soaking liquid. Rinse mushrooms in colander. Set aside.

In a saucepan, brown shallots lightly in 1 tablespoon butter; add garlic, red wine, tarragon, thyme and bay leaf. Boil rapidly to reduce liquid to about ⅓ cup. Add stock and 1 cup morel soaking liquid. (Discard any grit at bottom of morel liquid.) Bring to a boil. Skim carefully. Reduce heat to low and boil slowly until the volume is approximately 1 ½ cups. Add port. Strain and set aside.

Season filet mignons with salt and pepper. Melt 1 ½ tablespoons butter and the oil in a large skillet; brown filets. Finish cooking filets in a 425°F. oven until medium rare, about 4 to 5 minutes, turning filets at least once. Remove filets from pan and keep warm. Pour off fat. Add 1 tablespoon butter to skillet and briefly sauté morels over high heat. Add the wine sauce to the mushrooms and whisk in cold butter, one piece at a time, until thoroughly mixed and sauce is glossy and thickened. To serve, place each filet on a plate, pour sauce over the meat and spoon mushrooms around meat. Place strips of cold salmon on filets. Makes 4 servings.

RED SWISS CHARD AND SPINACH SAUTE

1 pound spinach leaves, ribs removed, and thoroughly washed
1 bunch red Swiss chard, ribs removed, and torn into 3-inch pieces
¼ pound butter
Freshly ground black pepper to taste

In a large pot bring to a boil 3 quarts water with 2 tablespoons salt. Blanch spinach and chard, in several batches, for 1 minute each batch. Immediately refresh the leaves in ice water or very cold water. Drain into a colander and squeeze the leaves dry by hand. Melt butter in a heavy saucepan, add the leaves and cook over low heat for 10 minutes, stirring, until vegetables absorb the butter and get meltingly soft. Season with pepper. Makes 4 servings.

ESPRESSO CREME CARAMEL

Caramel (following)
6 eggs
3 egg yolks
1 ¼ cups sugar
3 cups milk
1 cup whipping cream
3 ounces coarsely ground espresso beans

First prepare Caramel. For custard, beat eggs and yolks together until light and gradually beat in the sugar, beating until a ribbon forms. In a saucepan, heat milk and cream until steaming, add the ground beans, and let infuse for 10 minutes. Strain through cheesecloth, discarding the beans, and whisk strained liquid into the ribboned sugar-egg mixture. Skim foam. Pour into the caramelized cups. Set cups in a baking pan and fill with hot water to halfway up the sides of the cups. Bake in a 350°F. oven for approximately 25 minutes, or until just set. Cool, then refrigerate. Turn out on individual plates and pour Caramel over the top. Makes 8 servings.

CARAMEL In a saucepan place 1 ¼ cups sugar and 1 tablespoon water and cook until dissolved. Boil until a dark caramel color. Immediately pour into 8 custard cups. Cool.

Robert Del Grande
CAFE ANNIE
Houston, Texas

Self-taught chef Robert Del Grande, 29, of the Cafe Annie in Houston, Texas, switched his career to food just two years ago, in 1982.

After earning a Ph.D. in biochemistry from the University of California, Riverside in 1981, Del Grande was considering postdoctorate work when he was sidetracked into the culinary field.

Following graduation, Del Grande took a summer job at the Cafe Annie for fun (and a little extra money). Finishing his dissertation had been exhausting and he wanted to spend some time with his fiancée who lived in Houston before immersing himself in science again. He had always been curious as to how restaurant kitchens operate and thought he could learn a few things about food as well.

What happened was unexpected, he explains. He became very involved in the restaurant as well as very interested in becoming a chef. Many changes have since occurred. He is now chef and general partner of Cafe Annie. His wife, Mimi, is the general manager and partner. He runs the kitchen, and she, the dining room.

Del Grande's interest in food developed early. For Del Grande and his family in Burlingame, California, good food and dinner were always a focal point. "Mom was a great cook and I ate so well at home," he remembers. It was a shock when he moved away to school and found that his friends lacked the cooking skills he took for granted. Because he couldn't stand their fare, he became the full-time chef for his roommates.

Although not a scientist now in the usual meaning, Del Grande treats the kitchen as a laboratory. He uses his training as a biochemist to further develop his culinary knowledge. "Chemistry is a powerful tool for understanding the interac-

tion of foods and especially sauces," he says. His strong sense of adventure and investigation, his curiosity for the unusual, and his ability to solve problems have benefited him in his work.

The bistro-like restaurant is located in a shopping complex. Dark wood, red banquettes, rosy clay walls and brass railings impart a relaxed atmosphere.

Specialties include mushrooms in brandy sauce; polenta with Texas hare chili; roasted sweet potato salad with pecans; sweetbreads with black beans and sweet chilies; grilled chicken breast with goat cheese, honey and fresh thyme; redfish in sesame seed crust with cilantro; and Texas Axis deer with pecans, cognac and cream. For dessert, the restaurant is renowned for its four-layer chocolate mousse cake.

A man of many talents, Del Grande illustrated his recipe contributions with detailed drawings of the dishes in pen and ink and colored pencils. He executes similar art for his kitchen associates to explain his new inspirations.

A SUMMER MENU

Warm Semolina Cakes
with Three Cheeses,
Sweet Red Pepper and Basil

Grilled King Salmon
with Chili Pepper Sauce and
Avocado Puree

Fresh Figs with Port
and Cream

WARM SEMOLINA CAKES WITH THREE CHEESES, SWEET RED PEPPER AND BASIL

2 cups milk
½ teaspoon salt
Pinch white pepper
Pinch freshly grated nutmeg
½ cup semolina
2 tablespoons butter
1 cup freshly grated Parmesan
  cheese
2 egg yolks
Butter
6 ounces chèvre in a log shape
  (Montrachet or California
  chèvre)

1 sweet red pepper, seeded
  and diced
¼ cup fresh basil, chopped or 1
  teaspoon dried basil
4 green onions, chopped
½ cup virgin olive oil
6 ounces mozzarella or
  Monterey jack cheese, grated

In a deep saucepan, combine the milk, salt, pepper and nutmeg. Bring to a boil and slowly add the semolina while stirring constantly. Stir over moderate heat until the semolina becomes very thick and "pulls" away from the sides of the pot. Remove from heat and stir in butter. Then add 2 tablespoons of the Parmesan cheese. Mix in egg yolks, one at a time. Turn into a bowl and refrigerate until cooled and set. By hand shape into a dozen balls and pat into 2 ½-inch cakes.

In a large skillet sauté semolina cakes in 2 tablespoons butter over moderate heat for about 2 minutes on each side or until golden brown. Remove to a baking pan and place a slice of goat cheese on top of each cake. Bake in a 350°F. oven until goat cheese is warm, about 3 to 4 minutes.

Meanwhile in a skillet sauté pepper, basil and green onions in olive oil until warm and the aroma of the peppers and basil is evident. To serve, place 2 semolina cakes on each plate and sprinkle with the grated mozzarella cheese. Spoon the warm olive oil-and-pepper mixture over the top of each cake. Sprinkle with remaining Parmesan cheese. Makes 6 servings.

GRILLED KING SALMON WITH CHILI PEPPER SAUCE AND AVOCADO PUREE

Avocado Puree (following)
1 cup dry white wine
2 tablespoons chopped shallots
1 cup Fish Stock (page 147)
1 ½ cups whipping cream
2 teaspoons powdered chilies
  (preferably ancho chilies)
2 tablespoons vermouth
2 tablespoons chopped cilantro
2 tablespoons butter
6 king salmon steaks or fillets
2 tablespoons melted butter or
  olive oil
Cilantro leaves for garnish

Prepare Avocado Puree. For Chili Pepper Sauce, in a saucepan combine wine and shallots and reduce to ¼ cup liquid. Add fish stock and reduce to ½ cup. Add cream, chilies and vermouth and boil gently to reduce until slightly thickened. Add cilantro and whisk in 2 tablespoons butter, a tablespoon at a time.

To cook salmon, brush fish with melted butter or oil and grill over a wood charcoal fire, or broil, just until fish is slightly translucent but warm in the center, about 2 to 3 minutes per side. Place on dinner plates and spoon over the Avocado Puree. Surround with Chili Pepper Sauce and garnish with cilantro leaves. Makes 6 servings.

AVOCADO PUREE Halve 2 avocados, remove pits and spoon meat into a bowl. Mash until fairly smooth and mix in 1 cubed sweet red pepper, 1 peeled, seeded and chopped tomato, 1 tablespoon lemon juice and 2 tablespoons chopped cilantro. Season with salt and pepper to taste. Cover with plastic wrap, resting it on the surface, and refrigerate.

FRESH FIGS WITH PORT AND CREAM

1 dozen large fresh figs
1 cup whipping cream
¼ cup vintage port
Sugar to taste
Mint leaves for garnish

Cut figs in quarters and arrange the sections in a circular pattern on dessert plates allowing two figs per plate. Whip cream until it begins to thicken slightly, add port slowly and sugar and continue to whip until the cream is the consistency of a sauce. Spoon sauce around the figs and garnish the center with mint leaves. Makes 6 servings.

AN AUTUMN DINNER

Salad of Mussels, Tart Apples and Spinach with Cider Vinegar Cream

Loin Lamb Chops with Ragout of Yellow Onions, Sweet Red Pepper and Watercress

Chocolate Cake with Pears and Walnuts

SALAD OF MUSSELS, TART APPLES AND SPINACH WITH CIDER VINEGAR CREAM

3 pounds mussels, scrubbed
  and debearded
1 cup dry white wine
¼ cup celery, minced
2 garlic cloves, minced
2 tablespoons chopped fresh
  parsley
3 tablespoons cider vinegar
3 tablespoons peanut, walnut
  or olive oil
½ cup whipping cream
Salt and freshly ground black
  pepper to taste
3 bunches spinach, thoroughly
  washed
3 green apples
4 green onions, chopped
1 medium carrot, julienned
3 tomatoes, peeled, seeded and
  chopped

In a large saucepot place the mussels, wine, celery, garlic and parsley. Cover, bring to a boil and steam 5 minutes or until the shells open. Remove from heat and let cool to room temperature.

Strain liquid into a saucepan and boil to reduce to ¼ cup. Remove half of the mussels from their shells. With the remaining half, pry one of the shells off leaving the mussel on the half shell.

Combine the reduced liquid from the mussels and the cider vinegar in a bowl. Whisk in oil and then the cream. Season with salt and pepper. If necessary, adjust the amount of vinegar.

Reserve about 30 of the best spinach leaves and arrange them in a star pattern on salad plates. Tear remaining spinach leaves into pieces. Halve, core and dice apples. Add the shelled mussels, apples and green onions to the bowl with the dressing and mix well. Add the torn spinach and carrot julienne and toss. Place a mound of salad in the center of each plate and surround with the mussels on the half shell. Garnish each plate with two small mounds of chopped tomato. Makes 6 servings.

NOTE If desired, omit mussels and surround spinach salad with oysters on the half shell.

LOIN LAMB CHOPS WITH RAGOUT OF YELLOW ONIONS, SWEET RED PEPPER AND WATERCRESS

3 medium yellow onions
4 tablespoons olive oil
½ cup dry white wine
1 ½ cups Veal or Beef Stock
  (page 147)
Pinch cinnamon
Pinch freshly grated nutmeg
1 ½ cups whipping cream
Salt and freshly ground black
  pepper to taste
12 loin lamb chops, well-
  trimmed
Freshly ground black pepper
1 large sweet red pepper,
  seeded and chopped for
  garnish
2 bunches watercress for
  garnish

Peel onions and cut in half lengthwise; then slice across the grain into thin strips. In a large skillet sauté onion in 2 tablespoons of the oil until transparent, about 2 minutes. Add wine and boil to reduce by half. Add stock, cinnamon and nutmeg and reduce slowly until about ¼ cup of the liquid remains. Add cream and simmer to reduce until the cream is slightly thickened. Season with salt and pepper. Set aside and keep warm.

Rub chops with black pepper and the remaining 2 tablespoons oil. Grill over mesquite charcoal or broil until done, allowing about 3 to 4 minutes per side for medium rare.

To serve, place 2 chops per plate with the flat part of the bone together in the center of the plate. Spoon onion ragout on the plate on both sides of the chops, allowing the cream to flow around the chops. Add small mounds of chopped sweet pepper on top of the onion ragout and place sprigs of watercress between the flat bones of the chops at the center of the plate. Makes 6 servings.

CHOCOLATE CAKE WITH PEARS AND WALNUTS

Poached Pears (following)
Chocolate Cream (following)
¼ pound butter
1 cup sugar
6 eggs, separated
⅓ cup all-purpose flour
⅓ cup cocoa powder
2 tablespoons brandy
Walnuts for garnish
Chocolate shavings for garnish
Confectioners' sugar for
  garnish

Prepare Poached Pears and Chocolate Cream. To prepare cake, in a bowl beat butter with an electric mixer until creamy and beat in sugar, mixing until light in color. Add egg yolks one at a time, mixing well after each addition. Sift together flour and cocoa. Slowly add the flour-cocoa mixture and the brandy and continue mixing until incorporated. Whip egg whites until stiff but not dry and fold in. Butter and flour a 9-inch springform pan. Pour in batter and bake in a 350°F. oven for 45 minutes or until the cake is slightly puffed and a toothpick inserted comes out clean. Let cool on a rack. When cool remove from pan.

Arrange cake on a serving plate and spread the Chocolate Cream over the top of cake. Lay poached pear halves on the Chocolate Cream, setting them firmly in place. Sprinkle with walnuts and chocolate shavings. Just before serving, slice, and sprinkle with confectioners' sugar. Makes 6 servings.

POACHED PEARS Peel 3 Bartlett or Bosc pears and cut in half. Place the pear halves in a saucepan and cover with water. Add ¼ cup sugar and 1 tablespoon lemon juice and bring the liquid to a simmer. Poach until pears are tender, about 10 to 15 minutes. Remove pears from the liquid and core with a spoon. Cool. Glaze rounded side of pears with 2 tablespoons melted currant jelly.

CHOCOLATE CREAM In a saucepan combine 1 cup whipping cream and 4 ounces chopped semisweet chocolate and heat just until chocolate is melted, stirring. Remove from heat and let cool to room temperature, stirring occasionally. Stir in 1 teaspoon brandy. Whip at high speed with an electric mixer until light and fluffy.

Margaret Fox
CAFE BEAUJOLAIS
Mendocino, California

Nestled amid rose gardens and a wildflower–strewn meadow in Mendocino is a charming yellow Victorian-style house that is home to the Cafe Beaujolais.

There its owner, the dynamic chef Margaret Fox, 32, sets forth tantalizing breakfasts, lunches and dinners featuring the local fresh bounty. Cafe Beaujolais breakfasts, starring Fox's omelets, waffles and specialty muffins, are particularly renowned.

Baking has always been Fox's passion. She grew up in El Cerrito, California, in a food-oriented environment. "Mom was curious and analytical. She would delve into two dozen cookbooks to seek out the preferred recipe, and in so doing, taught me a lot by example," recalls Fox.

After receiving a bachelor's degree in psychology from the University of California, Santa Cruz, she realized a career in that field would require study at the graduate level, taking her another step away from her first love, baking. Her desire for tranquility and her need for temporary employment led her to Mendocino, a town she had heard about and thought sounded wonderful. She was hired as a baker at the Mendocino Hotel and she spent nine months in their kitchen. After having her fill of baking tarts, she left to work in a cheese shop and pursue more personal creative endeavors. She began to sell her own custom pastries and confections as a sideline.

Acquiring a restaurant happened spontaneously. When the established Cafe Beaujolais became available in 1976, Fox emptied her bank account and with two partners bought the business. Within two years she was sole proprietor, buying out her partners.

Her success and love for baking have prompted her into side ventures: launching a wholesale bakery business and marketing Panforte di Siena, an Italian nut confection, through mail order and specialty food shops nationwide. The candy now comes in four nut flavors: almond, hazelnut, walnut and macadamia nut.

The decor of the homey dining room complements the structure's nineteenth-century architecture. Flower-sprigged wallpaper, bare wood floors, assorted antique chairs and tables and miniature bouquets of field flowers impart an old-fashioned, country atmosphere.

Appetizers at dinner might be smoked salmon and caviar served with mascarpone and bialy (a homemade onion roll) or cold noodles tossed with mesquite-grilled chicken, cashews and peach vinegar. Entrées include roast duck with brandy and raspberries; poached salmon with zinfandel and tomato sauce; chicken quenelles; or snapper en papillotte. The White Mountain ice cream freezer churns out flavors of the season and there is always the house herb bread, baked three dozen at a time.

AN EASY SUMMER DINNER

Zucchini Curry Soup

An Unnamed Chicken Dish

Saffron Rice

Tahitian Vanilla Ice Cream

ZUCCHINI CURRY SOUP

1 large onion, chopped
2 teaspoons curry powder
1 tablespoon butter
4 zucchini, thickly sliced
3 cups Rich Chicken Stock
  (page 147)
¾ cup half-and-half
Salt and freshly ground black
  pepper to taste
Whipped Crème Fraîche for
  garnish (page 146)
Chopped chives (and chive
  blossoms, if available) for
  garnish

In a large soup pot sauté onion and curry powder in butter until onion is translucent, about 3 to 4 minutes. Add zucchini and stock. Cover, bring to a boil, and simmer 25 minutes, stirring occasionally.

Puree in a blender; strain. Add half-and-half and salt and pepper. Serve hot with a dollop of whipped crème fraîche and a sprinkling of chopped chives and a chive blossom per bowl. Makes 4 to 6 servings.

AN UNNAMED CHICKEN DISH

1 chicken, cut up
⅓ cup olive oil
4 garlic cloves, minced
1 large onion, finely chopped
¾ cup dry white wine
Salt and freshly ground black
 pepper to taste
½ lemon, thinly sliced and
 seeded
12 Italian dried olives
4 sun-dried tomatoes (pumate),
 chopped in small pieces*

Wash chicken and pat dry. In a large skillet heat oil, add chicken, skin side down, and sauté for 10 minutes. Turn and continue cooking for another 5 minutes. Remove from pan and keep warm. Add garlic and onion to remaining oil and cook over medium heat for about 5 minutes, or until onion is tender. Turn up heat, add wine and all the chicken pieces except the breast. Season with salt and pepper, cover and simmer for 15 minutes over medium heat. Turn pieces, add breasts, the lemon slices, olives and tomatoes. Replace cover and cook for an additional 10 to 15 minutes. Remove chicken to individual plates, quickly reduce liquid until syrupy and spoon over chicken, dividing olives, tomatoes and lemon slices evenly. Makes 4 servings.

Available at gourmet markets.

TAHITIAN VANILLA ICE CREAM

2 cups half-and-half
2 ½ cups whipping cream
½ split vanilla bean
1 cup plus 2 tablespoons sugar
10 egg yolks
1 ½ teaspoons vanilla extract

In a heavy saucepan heat until scalding the half-and-half, whipping cream and vanilla bean. Remove from heat and let steep for ½ hour. Place in a blender and blend until as smooth as possible. Then coarsely strain, retaining as much bean as possible in the liquid. Beat the egg yolks until thick and light in color, add the sugar and beat about 3 minutes. Reheat vanilla cream mixture and pour in. Return to a double boiler and cook, stirring constantly, over hot water, until custard coats a spoon. Remove from heat and immediately pour into a bowl placed over ice. Stir and add vanilla extract. Refrigerate until cold. Churn in an ice cream freezer following manufacturer's instructions until frozen. Makes about 2 quarts.

A SEPTEMBER DINNER

Caesar Salad of Romaine
with Garlic Croutons

Mendocino Fish Stew

Herb Bread

Cantaloupe Sorbet

MENDOCINO FISH STEW

⅔ cup finely chopped red
  onion
⅓ cup olive oil
4 garlic cloves, minced
1 ½ pounds rock cod or other
  firm-fleshed white fish, cut in
  1 ½ -inch squares
1 cup dry white wine
1 ½ cups tomato puree
2 tablespoons minced fresh
  basil or 1 ½ teaspoons dried
  basil
4 teaspoons green peppercorns
12 pimiento-stuffed olives,
  halved
12 Mediterranean black olives,
  pitted, halved
1 tablespoon capers (optional)

4 boiled red potatoes, kept
  warm
¼ cup minced fresh parsley
Lemon wedges for garnish
Sprigs of thyme (or thyme
  flowers, if available) for
  garnish

In a large skillet sauté onion
in oil until translucent; add
garlic and stir briefly over
high heat. Add fish to pan,
do not crowd, and continue
to cook over high heat,
turning pieces of fish, just
until they turn white on all
sides. Pour in wine and over
high heat reduce liquid for
about 1 minute. Add tomato
puree, basil, peppercorns,
olives and capers, if desired,
and heat through. Cut
potatoes into large cubes and
divide among four bowls.

Ladle fish and liquid over the
potatoes. Sprinkle with
minced parsley, tuck a lemon
wedge in the side of each
bowl and garnish with a
sprig of thyme or thyme
flowers. Makes 4 servings.

CANTALOUPE SORBET

1 cup water
¾ cup sugar
4 cups puree from very ripe
  cantaloupe, chilled
2 egg whites
Mint sprigs for garnish

In a small saucepan boil water
and sugar together for 5 minutes without stirring; cool. Mix
with chilled puree. Beat egg
whites until soft peaks form,
and fold in. Churn in an ice
cream freezer following manufacturer's instructions until frozen. Garnish each serving with
a sprig of mint. Makes about
1 ¾ quarts.

James Murcko
CAFE BEDFORD
San Francisco, California

The Cafe Bedford is part of a newly refurbished small hotel on Post Street near the fashionable Union Square shopping area in San Francisco. In the elegant but relaxed dining room, pale gray walls are offset by pale pink tablecloths and napkins. Black ceramic vases show off pink lilies at each table while a striking bouquet of multicolored blossoms centers the dessert display. Art deco plaster detail enhances the doorways. Skylights and the high ceiling lend a sense of spaciousness.

James Murcko, 25, the restaurant's first chef, works with all fresh ingredients, including such exotics as Swedish reindeer, Hawaiian opaka paka and Oregon morels, and choice Napa Valley herbs and cold-pressed olive oils.

The cuisine reflects the seasons and emphasizes quickly grilled meats and fish with light sauces. A first course

might be poached sea scallops with diced tomato, circled with sliced shiitake mushrooms and whimsical enokis; or a Mediterranean salad of grilled red pepper and eggplant, tiny Niçoise olives and spinach cloaked in feta cheese and herb dressing. Other choices include a warm duck salad and fettuccine tossed with smoked salmon and capers.

Entrées include sautéed veal glazed with cassis-flavored raspberry vinegar sauce, accompanied with caramelized shallots; whole trout stuffed with pecans and ham; and lamb roasted with herbs.

Standouts on the dessert table are raspberry tart with kiwi and apricots, apricot Grand Marnier sorbet and a dark chocolate cake showered with chocolate curls.

Murcko, a Connecticut native, decided in high school to become a chef. He attended the Culinary Institute of America in Hyde Park, New York. Before Cafe Bedford, he worked at the private Bohemian Club and the University Club in San Francisco.

A WINTER DINNER

Calamari Stuffed
with Basil-Shiitake Duxelle

Cranberry-Bourbon Sorbet

Braised Rabbit with Currants

Brussels Sprouts and Sautéed
Sweet Potato Balls

Hazelnut Cheesecake

CALAMARI STUFFED WITH BASIL-SHIITAKE DUXELLE*

18 whole fresh calamari
¾ pound shiitake mushrooms
2 shallots
½ cup packed basil leaves
2 tablespoons fresh parsley
¼ pound unsalted butter
3 tablespoons dry white wine
Salt and freshly ground black
   pepper to taste
3 tablespoons dry vermouth
2 garlic cloves, mashed
6 basil leaves

Clean calamari; save tentacles. In a food processor finely chop the mushrooms, shallots, basil and parsley. In a skillet sauté the mixture in 2 tablespoons butter and white wine for 2 minutes. Season with salt and pepper. Cool. Stuff calamari sacs ¾ full with mushroom mixture using a small spoon. Secure ends with toothpicks. Place calamari sacs and tentacles in a large sauté pan. Add 2 tablespoons butter, the vermouth and garlic. Cover, bring to a boil on top of the stove, then bake in a 350°F. oven for 5 minutes. To serve, arrange 3 sacs and tentacles on each plate; remove toothpicks. Return sauté pan to stove top. Over high heat whip in remaining butter in pieces, one piece at a time. Season with salt and pepper. Pour sauce over calamari. Garnish with basil. Makes 6 servings.

Duxelle is a reduction of finely minced mushrooms, shallots and seasonings.

CRANBERRY-BOURBON SORBET

1 cup sugar
3 cups water
3 tablespoons bourbon
1 pound fresh or frozen
   cranberries (thawed, if frozen)
Juice of ½ lemon

Combine sugar, water and bourbon in a saucepan. Bring to a boil. Add cranberries and simmer 4 to 5 minutes or until cranberries are soft. Puree mixture in a food processor; strain and cool. Churn in an ice cream freezer following manufacturer's instructions until frozen. Makes about 1 ¼ quarts.

BRAISED RABBIT WITH CURRANTS

1 large rabbit (about 3 ½
   pounds), cut into 6 pieces
3 tablespoons seasoned all-
   purpose flour
3 tablespoons vegetable oil
¾ cup Demi-Glace (page 148)
1 cup zinfandel or other dry
   red wine
½ cup currants
2 tablespoons raisins
1 small onion, diced
2 tablespoons cognac or brandy
Salt and freshly ground black
   pepper to taste
Brussels sprouts and sautéed
   sweet potato balls for
   accompaniment

Dust rabbit with seasoned flour
and shake off. In a large skillet
brown rabbit in hot oil on all
sides. Remove from pan to an
ovenproof casserole. Add to
the skillet the demi-glace,
wine, ¼ cup of the currants,
raisins and onion and bring to
a boil. Pour over browned rabbit, cover, and bake in a 325°F.
oven for 50 minutes, or until
tender. Remove from oven and
let sit 15 minutes.

Transfer rabbit to a hot platter and pour sauce into a food
processor; puree and strain. If
necessary, reduce sauce in a
saucepan until it coats a spoon.
Heat remaining ¼ cup currants
in cognac until the alcohol is
burned off. Add to sauce and
season with salt and pepper.
Return rabbit to sauce, reheat
and serve. Accompany with
Brussels sprouts and sautéed
sweet potato balls, if desired.
Makes 6 servings.

HAZELNUT CHEESECAKE

Amaretto cookies or almond
   macaroons
⅔ cup hazelnuts, roasted and
   skins rubbed off
4 eggs
½ cup plus 2 tablespoons sugar
1 teaspoon vanilla extract
½ cup frangelico or amaretto
1 teaspoon grated lemon peel
1 ½ pounds natural cream
   cheese, at room temperature
1 cup sour cream

Space 8 amaretto cookies
around the sides of a buttered
10-inch springform pan. In a
food processor, grind enough
remaining cookies to make ⅔
cup crumbs. Grind hazelnuts
finely and mix with the cookie
crumbs. Coat the bottom of the
pan with half of the amaretto-
nut mixture.

Beat eggs until blended and
beat in ½ cup of the sugar, vanilla, 6 tablespoons of the liqueur and the lemon peel. In a
separate bowl cream cheese
until light and fluffy and gradually beat in the egg-sugar mixture, beating until smooth.
Pour batter into the crumb-
lined pan. Bake in a 350°F. oven
for 20 minutes or until barely
set. Blend together the sour
cream, remaining 2 table-
spoons sugar and 2 table-
spoons liqueur. Spread over
top of cheesecake and sprinkle
with remaining amaretto-nut
mixture. Continue baking 5
minutes longer. Let cool. Refrigerate. Makes 8 servings.

A SUMMER BARBECUE DINNER

Cold Tomato Bisque with Basil Sorbet

Grilled Tuna with Marinated Tomatillos

Sautéed Zucchini

Lemon Curd Tarts with Berries

COLD TOMATO BISQUE WITH BASIL SORBET

Basil Sorbet (following)
1 small onion, diced
⅓ green pepper, diced
1 small celery stalk, diced
2 large garlic cloves, minced
2 tablespoons olive oil
2 pounds tomatoes, peeled, seeded and quartered
⅓ cup dry red wine
2 tablespoons white wine vinegar
2 ½ cups Chicken Stock (page 147)
2 sprigs fresh thyme or ½ teaspoon dried thyme
2 teaspoons chopped fresh basil or ½ teaspoon dried basil
2 teaspoons chopped fresh oregano or ½ teaspoon dried oregano
1 small bay leaf
½ cup whipping cream
Salt and freshly ground black pepper to taste
2 tablespoons fresh lemon juice
Basil sprigs for garnish

Prepare Basil Sorbet. In a large saucepot sauté onion, pepper, celery and garlic in oil over low heat, stirring, until onion is transparent. Add tomatoes and cook 5 minutes. Add wine and vinegar and cook 2 minutes. Add stock, thyme, basil, oregano and bay leaf. Cover and simmer 15 minutes.

Remove from heat. Remove thyme and bay leaf. Puree in a blender or food processor. Refrigerate until cool, then add cream, salt and pepper and lemon juice. Refrigerate until serving time. To serve, ladle soup into bowls and top each with a scoop of Basil Sorbet. Garnish with a sprig or leaf of basil. Makes 6 servings.

BASIL SORBET In a food processor puree ¾ cup tightly packed basil leaves, 1 clove garlic, 1 ½ tablespoons freshly grated Parmesan cheese, 2 teaspoons lemon juice, 2 teaspoons olive oil and 3 tablespoons dry white wine (alcohol burned off). Add ⅔ cup water and 1 slightly beaten egg white. Turn into a metal container and freeze until slushy. Transfer to a food processor and process until light and fluffy. Return to the freezer to harden. Makes 1 ½ cups.

GRILLED TUNA WITH MARINATED TOMATILLOS

1 pound tomatillos, peeled and
  thinly sliced*
1 small red onion, quartered
  and sliced
Juice and peel of 1 lime
1 jalapeño pepper, seeded and
  finely chopped
1 tablespoon chopped fresh
  basil or ¾ teaspoon dried basil
1 tablespoon chopped fresh
  cilantro
1 tomato, diced
5 tablespoons olive oil
2 tablespoons white wine
  vinegar
¼ teaspoon ground cumin
Salt and freshly ground black
  pepper to taste
6 portions of tuna or shark (5 to
  6 ounces each)
3 tablespoons fresh lemon juice
⅓ cup chopped fresh herbs:
  tarragon, basil, thyme,
  parsley, chives (combination
  or parsley and chives)

In a bowl mix together the to-matillos, onion, lime juice and peel, jalapeño pepper, basil, cilantro, tomato, 1 tablespoon of the olive oil, vinegar, cumin and salt and pepper. Cover and refrigerate 2 hours.

About 20 minutes before grilling, marinate the fish in the remaining olive oil, lemon juice and chopped fresh herbs. Grill fish over hot coals allow-ing about 2 minutes on each side, basting frequently with olive oil and lemon juice mari-nade. Serve hot grilled fish on a bed of cold tomatillo mixture. Makes 6 servings.

Available at Latino and specialty produce markets.

LEMON CURD TARTS WITH BERRIES

Individual Tart Shells
  (following)
2 eggs
5 egg yolks
1 cup sugar
⅔ cup fresh lemon juice
1 tablespoon grated lemon peel
1 tablespoon dry white wine
1 tablespoon butter
Blueberries, raspberries or
  blackberries for garnish

Prepare Individual Tart Shells. For filling, in a double boiler beat eggs and egg yolks until blended. Mix in sugar, lemon juice, lemon peel and wine. Cook over hot water, stirring constantly, until thickened. Re-move from heat and stir in but-ter. Cool. Fill tart shells and garnish with berries just before serving. Makes 6 servings.

INDIVIDUAL TART SHELLS In a heavy duty mixer or by hand, beat ½ pound butter and ¼ cup sugar until light and creamy. Add 1 egg plus 1 egg yolk and mix well. Add 2 ½ cups flour and mix on low speed just until incorporated. Don't overmix. Chill dough 1 hour. Roll out ⅛ -inch thick and cut out rounds to fit 4-inch tart pans with re-movable bottoms. Press dough rounds into tart pans. Chill un-til firm. Line dough with foil and fill with beans. Bake in a 400°F. oven for 15 minutes; re-move foil and beans, reduce oven to 350°F. and bake 10 min-utes longer or until golden brown. Cool. Remove shells from pans. Makes about 8 tarts.

Franklin Biggs
CAFE MARIPOSA
Silver Lake Lodge
Deer Valley Resort
Park City, Utah

Halfway up a ski mountain in Park City, Utah, at 8,200 feet, stands the Silver Lake Lodge where Executive Chef Franklin Biggs, 29, oversees the kitchen of the sophisticated Cafe Mariposa and the informal Snuggery, all part of the elite Deer Valley Resort. Recently he was named lodge manager as well.

The informally elegant Cafe Mariposa, open only for dinner, glows with a welcoming friendliness by lamp and firelight. Redwood walls, rust tablecloths and candle-lit hurricane globes wreathed with pink lilies lend rustic accents. The menu reflects a French in-

fluence with some nouvelle touches that typifies Biggs's approach to cuisine. His food is innovative yet soundly based on classical concepts. The thrust is international, drawing on the best fresh ingredients from around the world. The flavors are also worldly, occasionally sparked by a Japanese touch.

Appetizers encompass smoked mountain trout with golden caviar sauce; Oriental pasta salad; cold linguine tossed with seasonal vegetables and slivers of poached chicken, dressed with sesame oil, soy and ginger; and salmon and scallop mousse with watercress mayonnaise.

Entrées include roast game hen au vinaigre, split and served with a tomato-vinegar concasse; rack of lamb al pesto; and roast tenderloin of beef rolled in crushed black peppercorns with red wine sauce.

Among the sweets are selections from the pastry table, a

potpourri of fresh fruit sorbets and a specialty: Trio of Ice Creams Mariposa, featuring chocolate, vanilla and praline ice creams capped by pistachio nut sauce.

Biggs's first success in the food world came at age sixteen selling fresh Dungeness crab at an outdoor stand at Fisherman's Wharf after school. He worked his way through the University of California, Berkeley, where he earned a degree in political science, by managing the faculty club.

Finished with college, Biggs tagged after a girlfriend to Paris and on a whim walked into the noted cooking school La Varenne. He stayed at the school for nine months as a student trainee and teaching assistant. Later, working at Maxim's and Taillevent, he gained more skills. He returned to California and jobs at several San Francisco restaurants and the UC faculty club before settling in Utah where his girlfriend had begun graduate studies and where he could ski.

According to Biggs, who has been at Deer Valley since it opened in December, 1981, the problems of working at a ski resort are mostly seasonal. During peak winter months, Biggs's staff of cooks swells to twenty-six. In the slower summer, only three are needed.

Biggs loves his stay at what he calls "the Cadillac of ski resorts," challenged by his work and the first class skiing available almost outside his door.

AN ALL-SEASONS MENU

Consommé Madrilene

Scallops in Puff Pastry with Ginger Beurre Blanc

Veal Medallions with Madeira Truffle Sauce

Green Salad

Marquise au Chocolat, Taillevent

SCALLOPS IN PUFF PASTRY WITH GINGER BEURRE BLANC

9 ounces Puff Pastry (page 150) or ½ package frozen puff pastry sheets, thawed
1 cup clam juice
½ cup dry white wine
¾ pound fresh scallops
Ginger Beurre Blanc (following)
3 green onions, slivered for garnish

Cut puff pastry into 6 diamond-shaped pieces, about 3 inches on each side. Arrange on a baking sheet. Bake in a 425°F. oven for 15 minutes or until puffed and golden brown. Split horizontally and keep warm. In a medium saucepan bring clam juice and wine to a boil. Add scallops and simmer gently 2 minutes, or until barely cooked through and still slightly translucent in the center. Prepare Ginger Beurre Blanc. For each serving, place pastry diamond bottom on a plate, arrange scallops in and around each, coat with sauce, sprinkle with green onions, and place pastry diamond top at a pleasing angle. Makes 6 first course servings.

GINGER BEURRE BLANC Finely chop 2 shallots. In a saucepan gently sauté chopped shallots with 3 tablespoons peeled and finely chopped ginger root in 1 tablespoon butter, cooking until soft but not brown. Add ⅓ cup dry white wine and ¼ cup Fish Stock (page 147) and boil until liquid is reduced to 2 tablespoons. Add 2 tablespoons whipping cream and reduce to 2 tablespoons. Over low heat whisk in ½ pound cold butter, cut in pieces, one piece at a time. Add salt and white pepper to taste; strain and serve.

VEAL MEDALLIONS WITH MADEIRA TRUFFLE SAUCE

1 ½ pounds veal cutlets or veal tenderloin, cut in 3 medallions per person
All-purpose flour
Clarified Butter (page 146)
⅓ cup Madeira
2 ¼ cups Demi-Glace, slightly thickened (page 148)
1 ½ tablespoons chopped truffle (optional)*
1 ½ tablespoons cold butter, cut in pieces
Salt and freshly ground black pepper to taste
Garnish: julienned truffles; 18 each potato ovals, turnip ovals and carrot ovals, each simmered until just tender; 6 fluted mushroom caps, poached; 1 bunch watercress

Dredge veal lightly in flour. In a large skillet sauté veal in about 2 tablespoons butter until golden brown on both sides. Deglaze pan with Madeira; flame. Remove veal and keep warm. Reduce Madeira to a glaze. Add demi-glace and truffles. Reduce by one-third. Whip in butter, one piece at a time, and adjust seasonings. To serve, arrange 3 veal medallions in the middle of each plate, nap with sauce, top with julienne of truffle, and surround with trios of vegetables. Between two vegetable trios nest a fluted mushroom in sprigs of watercress. Makes 6 servings.

Available at gourmet markets.

MARQUISE AU CHOCOLAT, TAILLEVENT*

6 ounces bittersweet chocolate, chopped
6 ounces semisweet chocolate, chopped
10 ounces unsalted butter, cut in pieces
⅞ cup confectioners' sugar, sifted
8 egg yolks
4 egg whites
½ cup whipping cream
Pistachio Crème Anglaise (following)

In a double boiler melt chocolates and butter over hot water. In a bowl mix sugar and egg yolks just until blended. Beat egg whites until stiff but not dry. Fold the yolk mixture into the slightly warm chocolate. Gently fold beaten egg whites into the mixture. Let cool to room temperature. Whip cream to soft peaks and fold into the chocolate mixture. Line bottom and sides of an 8-by-4-inch loaf pan with buttered parchment and pour mixture into prepared pan. Cover with plastic wrap and refrigerate overnight. Unmold by dipping in warm water and running a hot knife around edge. Peel off parchment. Cut in ⅓-inch-thick slices and serve on a pool of Pistachio Crème Anglaise. Makes about 2 dozen servings.

PISTACHIO CREME ANGLAISE
Scald 1 quart whole milk with 1 split vanilla bean. Beat 12 egg yolks until light and beat in 2 cups sugar. Pour in part of the milk and stir to blend. In a double boiler, blend yolk mixture into the remaining scalded milk and cook over hot water, stirring, until custard coats a spoon. Remove from heat and cool in a pan of ice water. Finely grind ½ pound roasted, unsalted pistachios in a food processor or blender. Stir the ground nuts into the crème anglaise and let steep 15 to 20 minutes. Strain, discarding nuts and vanilla bean. Refrigerate. Makes about 2 quarts.

*A Marquise is a French-style dessert loaf. It will keep refrigerated up to 1 week or it may be frozen for serving on more than one occasion.

Bradley Ogden
CAMPTON PLACE
RESTAURANT
San Francisco, California

A decidedly American menu awaits the diner at the elegant new Campton Place Restaurant under the guiding hand of a young and personable midwesterner, Bradley Ogden, 30.

The fare reflects Ogden's roots in the nation's heartland expressed with a light, clear and emphatically creative touch, while also drawing on the best and freshest ingredients from throughout America.

Ogden readily belongs to the new breed of American chefs. An identical twin in a family of seven children, he grew up in the resort town of Traverse City, Michigan. His father loved to cook and young Ogden often assisted. Fudge, chocolate cakes and peach and banana ice cream were Ogden family favorites.

Ogden attended the Culinary Institute of America, graduating with honors and was named "most-likely-to-succeed." Returning to his native Midwest, he worked at a number of resorts and restaurants before overseeing the American Restaurant at Crown Center, Kansas City, a consistent Mobil four-star winner.

At his new post in California, Ogden has the freedom to create a menu in his own style.

Specialties include dollar-sized blue corn cakes topped with coral spiny lobsters, smoked duck salad with roasted peppers and pheasant swathed in a grape and pecan sauce served with fluffy spoonbread. Desserts include a flourless pecan chocolate cake, double crust apple pie, six nut torte, silken vanilla bean ice cream and raspberry sorbet.

The sophisticated dining room at Campton Place, sheathed floor-to-ceiling in muted apricot fabric, is a refined backdrop for Ogden's culinary flair. Taupe upholstered chairs with fruitwood arms provide cushioned seating. A beige marble buffet backed by glass etched with a swan makes a captivating sideboard to display desserts and show off dramatic floral arrangements. Antique celadon plates and ginger jars further accent the decor.

A family man with three young sons, Ogden leaves the cooking at home to his wife and joins his boys over hamburgers and hot dogs.

AN EARLY SUMMER MENU

Crab Chowder

Duck, Orange and Avocado Salad

Strawberry Sorbet

CRAB CHOWDER

Cooked 3-pound Dungeness crab (following)
½ cup salt pork, rind removed, and diced
½ cup bacon, diced
2 cups chopped onions
1 ½ cups diced celery
1 tablespoon fresh thyme or ¾ teaspoon dried thyme
½ cup all-purpose flour
3 cups whipping cream
2 cups peeled, diced Idaho potatoes, blanched in lightly salted water
1 tablespoon kosher salt
1 teaspoon ground white pepper
½ teaspoon Tabasco sauce
Chopped parsley for garnish

Cook the crab, reserving the poaching liquid. In a heavy pot place the salt pork and bacon and cook over high heat until the meat is crispy and the fat is rendered. Pour off most of the fat. Add onions and celery and sauté over medium heat for about 8 minutes or until the vegetables are tender. Stir in thyme and flour to make a roux. Cook at low heat for 5 minutes. Slowly add approximately 2 quarts poaching liquid from the crab, stirring constantly, until all the liquid has been absorbed. Simmer 20 minutes. Add the cream, potatoes, salt, pepper and Tabasco and heat through. Just before serving, add the crab meat. Garnish with parsley. Makes 12 servings.

POACHED DUNGENESS CRAB In a stock pot combine 2 quarts clam juice, 1 cup sherry, ½ cup brandy, 8 parsley stems, 4 bay leaves, ¼ cup minced shallots and 1 tablespoon minced garlic cloves. Bring to a boil, add 1 whole live Dungeness crab (about 3 pounds) and simmer 12 to 15 minutes, or until crab is done. Remove crab from liquid; let cool slightly. Crack and bone crab leaving the meat in large pieces; set aside. Strain poaching liquid through a fine strainer or cheesecloth and reserve for soup with crabmeat.

DUCK, ORANGE AND AVOCADO SALAD

Orange Dressing (following)
2 heads bibb lettuce
1 bunch spinach (about 2 dozen leaves)
¼ cup coarsely chopped cilantro leaves
1 large duck, poached, skin removed and meat cut into ⅜ - inch slices (or substitute a 3-pound roasted chicken)

2 navel oranges, sectioned
2 avocados
¼ cup julienned orange zest, blanched in boiling water 5 minutes and drained

Prepare Orange Dressing. For salad, toss bibb lettuce, spinach leaves and cilantro with ¼ cup dressing. Mix duck slices with ¼ cup dressing. On a large platter or individual plates arrange the greens and duck. Top with alternating sections of orange and sliced avocado. Sprinkle with orange zest strips. Makes 4 servings.

ORANGE DRESSING Whisk together in a bowl 1 teaspoon Dijon-style mustard, 1 teaspoon freshly grated orange zest, 1 egg yolk, ½ teaspoon kosher salt, 2 tablespoons red wine vinegar, 2 tablespoons fresh orange juice and 8 tablespoons olive oil. Chill until serving time.

STRAWBERRY SORBET

⅔ cup sugar
⅔ cup water
3 cups strawberry puree (about 3 pints strawberries)
4 tablespoons fresh lemon juice
2 egg whites

Prepare a simple syrup by combining sugar and water in a saucepan. Bring to a boil, remove from heat and let cool. Combine the sugar syrup, strawberry puree, and lemon juice and chill. Beat egg whites until frothy and fold into strawberry mixture. Churn in an ice cream freezer following manufacturer's instructions until frozen. Makes about 1 quart.

AN ALL-SEASONS DINNER

Wild Mushrooms in an Herb Crust

Veal Medallions Stuffed with Herbed Cheese

Six Nut Torte

WILD MUSHROOMS IN AN HERB CRUST

3 tablespoons shallots, minced
2 tablespoons unsalted butter
2 garlic cloves, minced
1 ½ cups quartered
 chanterelles (stems removed)*
1 ½ cups quartered shiitake
 mushrooms (stems removed)*
1 ½ cups oyster mushrooms
 (stems removed)*
⅓ cup dry sherry
¼ cup Madeira
1 ½ cups whipping cream
½ teaspoon ground white
 pepper
1 teaspoon kosher salt
Herb Crust (following)

In a large skillet over medium heat sauté shallots in butter 2 minutes or until translucent. Add garlic and sauté another minute. Add mushrooms and sauté 5 to 7 minutes. Add sherry, Madeira, cream, pepper and salt; cook 5 minutes longer. With a slotted spoon remove mushrooms to a bowl. Continue to cook sauce until it is reduced and coats the back of a spoon, about 10 minutes.

Add mushrooms back into the sauce and spoon into 4 buttered 8-ounce ovenproof dishes. Top each with Herb Crust and brown quickly under the broiler or brown in a 450°F. oven for about 5 minutes. Makes 4 servings.

HERB CRUST Mix together ½ cup fresh white bread crumbs, ½ cup freshly grated Parmesan cheese, ½ cup grated Gruyère cheese, 3 tablespoons chopped fresh parsley, 1 tablespoon chopped fresh basil and 1 teaspoon chopped fresh thyme.

*Available at specialty produce or gourmet markets. If desired, substitute 4 ½ cups quartered domestic mushrooms.

VEAL MEDALLIONS STUFFED WITH HERBED CHEESE

Basil-Lemon Sauce (following)
1 cup farmer's cheese, diced or
 4 ounces natural cream cheese
½ cup domestic provolone
 cheese, diced or Jarlsberg or
 Gruyère
¼ cup chopped fresh basil, or 2
 teaspoons dried basil
1 tablespoon chopped fresh
 thyme or ½ teaspoon dried
 thyme
1 tablespoon chopped fresh
 marjoram or ½ teaspoon dried
 marjoram
1 tablespoon chopped fresh
 oregano or ½ teaspoon dried
 oregano
8 slices veal round (2 ounces
 each), pounded ⅛-inch thick
Seasoned all-purpose flour
2 tablespoons vegetable oil or
 Clarified Butter (page 146)
12 basil leaves for garnish

Prepare Basil-Lemon Sauce. For filling, mix together the cheeses, basil, thyme, marjoram and oregano. Place 2 or 3 tablespoons on the center of each piece of veal and roll, making certain the ends are tucked in. Secure with string or a toothpick. Dust with seasoned flour.

In a large skillet heat oil or butter until very hot. Place meat rolls in pan sealed side down and cook until golden brown, turning. Place skillet in a 400°F. oven for about 3 minutes or until cooked through. To serve, arrange two medallions on each plate, garnish with 3 basil leaves and spoon over Basil-Lemon Sauce. Makes 4 servings.

BASIL-LEMON SAUCE Place in a saucepan 1 cup dry white wine, ½ cup fresh basil stems and leaves and 2 tablespoons minced shallots. Bring to a boil and reduce by half. Strain through a sieve and return to low heat. Slowly blend in ¾ cup unsalted butter, at room temperature in pieces, one piece at a time. Remove from heat and add ½ teaspoon kosher salt, ¼ teaspoon ground white pepper and the juice of two lemons.

SIX NUT TORTE

Almond Crust (following)
1 ¾ cups mixed nuts: pecans, walnut halves, roasted filberts, whole macadamias, roasted pistachios and whole almonds
4 tablespoons unsalted butter
1 cup firmly packed dark brown sugar
½ cup light corn syrup
3 eggs
½ teaspoon vanilla extract
1 tablespoon brandy
Whipped cream for garnish

Prepare Almond Crust. Toast nuts on a baking pan in a 350°F. oven 8 to 10 minutes. For filling, cream butter and sugar thoroughly. Add corn syrup and mix in. Add eggs, one at a time, beating well after each addition. Stir in vanilla and brandy. Reserve ⅓ cup of the nuts for decoration and stir remainder into the filling. Turn into chilled pastry. Top with reserved nuts arranged in concentric circles. Bake in a 375°F. oven for 35 to 40 minutes or until filling is set. Cool. Serve cut in wedges with a dollop of unsweetened whipped cream. Makes 10 servings.

ALMOND CRUST In a food processor combine ½ cup finely ground almonds and ½ cup finely ground filberts with ½ cup confectioners' sugar. With a mixer, cream ¼ cup unsalted butter. Mix in the sugar and nut mixture and ⅔ cup cake flour. Add 1 egg yolk and mix until dough clings together. Pat into a ball, wrap in plastic wrap and refrigerate 1 hour. Roll out dough and line a 9-inch tart pan with removable bottom. Refrigerate before baking.

**Robert Brody
CHAMBRETTE
Sheraton Harbor Island West
San Diego, California**

"Food should be fun, full of life and gusto," says Robert Brody, 39, the executive chef of the newly opened Chambrette Restaurant in San Diego.

For Chambrette, Brody has styled a menu of "earthy, simplistic dishes with depth—like composed cassoulets and choucroutes." He believes that nouvelle cuisine made a statement, but it's time to head back toward Grandma's cooking, a tribute perhaps to the talents of his own Russian grandmother. Brody says her interpretation of such classics of Jewish cooking as chicken soup and knishes made an indelible mark on his childhood palate.

A New Yorker, Brody earned a master's degree in education at the State University of New York in Albany after serving as a VISTA volunteer in West Virginia. He then spent two years traveling in Europe, Africa and Asia. When he returned to the States he worked as a hotel waiter for two years to save money to go abroad again. He had read about La Varenne Cooking School and when he arrived in Paris, he went to the school "to learn to cook." After a year of training he apprenticed at a two-star Michelin restaurant, Chateau du Locqunole in Brittany.

After three years in France, Brody returned to this country to work, first at the Greenhouse in Cohassett, Massachusetts, and then at a resort on Nantucket where "everything was fresh fish." With Sheraton, he opened Apley's, Sheraton's signature (top) restaurant in Boston, before coming to San Diego and the West Coast Sheraton Harbor Island East, and then on to Sheraton Harbor Island West.

The decor of Chambrette, a spacious 150-seat restaurant, is a wash of gray and rose. Tall French doors open onto a garden terrace. Beyond is a marina where boats at anchor add to the picturesque vista.

Specialties of Chambrette include seafood cassoulet, leeks and escargot in honey cider vinegar, shrimp tortellini with lobster sauce and warm pear tart.

A SPRING THROUGH SUMMER DINNER

Westphalian Pheasant Salad

Ragout of Veal and Lamb Sweetbreads
with Lobster and Asparagus

Fresh Noodles

Hot Green Beans

White Chocolate Mousse with Fresh Raspberry Sauce

WESTPHALIAN PHEASANT SALAD

2 ounces Westphalian ham, sliced medium-thick
1 whole pheasant breast, split
1 bunch spinach, washed and torn into pieces
1 bunch chicory, cleaned and torn
½ cup white corn kernels (optional)
Sesame Dressing (following)
2 tablespoons toasted chopped hazelnuts

Wrap a ham slice around each pheasant breast. Grill or broil about 8 minutes or until cooked through. Remove ham and cut the breasts into a thin julienne. In a bowl mix the spinach and chicory. Add the corn, if desired, and pheasant. Pour over the Sesame Dressing and mix lightly. Divide the mixture on four plates and sprinkle with hazelnuts. Makes 4 servings.

SESAME DRESSING In a bowl whisk together 2 egg yolks and beat in ½ cup sesame oil,* 6 tablespoons peanut oil, 2 tablespoons apple cider vinegar, 2 tablespoons honey, 1 tablespoon Dijon-style mustard and 1 tablespoon toasted sesame seeds (optional), beating until emulsified.

*Available at Oriental markets.

RAGOUT OF VEAL AND LAMB SWEETBREADS WITH LOBSTER AND ASPARAGUS

Poaching Liquid (following)
Court Bouillon (following)
1 pound Veal Sweetbreads, soaked, blanched and cleaned (page 148)
1 pound Lamb Sweetbreads, soaked, blanched and cleaned (page 148)
2 lobster tails
1 quart Veal Stock (page 147)
1 cup whipping cream
Salt
Dash cayenne pepper
2 dozen asparagus spears
Butter

Prepare Poaching Liquid and Court Bouillon. Cook veal and lamb sweetbreads in Poaching Liquid for 15 minutes or until cooked through. Let cool in liquid. Strain and reserve 1 cup liquid. Drain sweetbreads, plunge in cold water and separate into small pieces, discarding any filament.

Skewer lobster tails along the top part of the shell to prevent the tail from curling and poach in Court Bouillon just until they turn pink, about 6 minutes. Cool. Strain and reserve 1 cup of stock.

In a saucepan, mix the strained cooking liquids from the sweetbreads and the lobster with the veal stock. Bring to a boil and simmer until reduced and it coats the back of a spoon, about 1 ½ cups. Add the cream and continue cooking until further reduced and slightly thickened. Season with salt and cayenne.

Cut the asparagus about ½ inch below the bottom of the tips. Cook the tips in boiling salted water just until crisply tender; drain and keep warm.

Slice the lobster into ¼-inch medallions and warm gently in butter. Add the sweetbreads to the sauce and spoon into a casserole dish. Garnish with the asparagus tips and lobster slices. Makes 4 servings.

POACHING LIQUID In a soup pot, combine 2 quartered onions, 2 carrots, 2 stalks celery, 1 crushed bay leaf and a small handful of juniper berries. Add ½ cup white wine vinegar and 1 ½ quarts water. Slowly bring to a boil and let simmer 15 minutes.

COURT BOUILLON Prepare as for Poaching Liquid, substituting black peppercorns for juniper berries.

WHITE CHOCOLATE MOUSSE WITH FRESH RASPBERRY SAUCE

¾ cup sugar
¼ cup water
½ cup egg whites
  (approximately 4)
¾ pound white chocolate, cut
  into shavings
1 pint whipping cream
Raspberry Sauce (following)

Place sugar and water in a saucepan and boil until the temperature reaches 238° (soft ball stage) on a candy thermometer. While sugar syrup is cooking, whip egg whites with an electric mixer until stiff peaks form and immediately pour the sugar syrup over the whites in a slow steady stream. Whip the mixture about 3 minutes; beat in the chocolate and continue beating until mixture cools to room temperature, about 7 minutes. When cool, whip cream until stiff and fold in. Turn into a dessert bowl and chill. Prepare Raspberry Sauce. To serve, spoon a portion of mousse on each plate. Surround mousse with a pool of Raspberry Sauce. Makes 8 to 10 servings.

RASPBERRY SAUCE Puree in a food processor 1 pint raspberries, 1 tablespoon sugar, 1 tablespoon kirsch and a pinch of salt. Strain through a fine sieve to remove seeds. Chill.

AN AUTUMN DINNER

Wild Mushroom Ravioli

Seafood Fruit de Mer

Green Salad

Crusty French Bread

Pears in Puff Pastry with Crème Anglaise

WILD MUSHROOM RAVIOLI

1 quart Veal Stock (page 147)
½ onion, peeled
1 medium carrot, peeled and
  halved
¼ pound unsalted butter,
  softened
2 pounds assorted wild
  mushrooms or domestic
  mushrooms, chopped*
½ cup whipping cream
Salt and freshly ground black
  pepper to taste
1 cup blanched chopped fresh
  spinach
32 wonton skins
Egg wash (1 egg beaten with 1
  tablespoon water)
Snipped fresh chives for
  garnish

Place the stock, onion and carrot in a saucepan and bring to a boil. Reduce to 1 cup, or until slightly thickened and discard vegetables. Melt 1 tablespoon of the butter in a skillet and sauté mushrooms over low heat until most of their liquid has been rendered. Remove from heat and pour the mushroom liquid into the veal stock. Add the cream to the mushrooms, return to heat and let reduce until the cream has become quite thick. When the sauce is reduced so that it easily coats the back of a spoon, remove from heat and whisk in remaining butter, one piece at a time. Keep warm. Season with salt and pepper and let cool. Mix in spinach.

Lay the wonton skins on a lightly floured board. Place a tablespoon of the mushroom mixture in the middle of each skin. Brush egg wash around the edge of each wonton and fold in half, forming a triangular package. Or, if desired bend each triangle around your finger, pressing 1 pointed end over the other like tortellini. Or, cut the wonton into circles and fold into half moons.

Steam or poach filled wontons in boiling salted water until skins are cooked through, about 5 minutes; drain. Add to hot sauce. Spoon onto plates and garnish with freshly snipped chives. Makes 4 servings.

Wild mushrooms are available at gourmet markets.

SEAFOOD FRUIT DE MER

3 shallots, minced
1 bouquet garni (3 sprigs fresh
  parsley, 1 bay leaf, 2 sprigs
  fresh thyme or ½ teaspoon
  dried thyme, in a cheesecloth
  bag)
2 cups dry white wine
12 mussels, scrubbed and
  debearded
8 medium shrimp, shelled and
  deveined
4 sole fillets (3 ounces each)
4 ounces halibut fillets, cut in
  strips
4 ounces rock cod, cut in
  chunks
8 scallops
12 new carrots, cleaned with
  ¼-inch stem left on, blanched
8 new turnips, cleaned and
  blanched
16 baby onions, blanched
1 leek (white part only),
  cleaned and chopped
½ pound butter, softened, cut
  in pieces
2 tablespoons chopped fresh
  tarragon or 1 ½ teaspoons
  dried tarragon

In a medium saucepan bring to a simmer the shallots, bouquet garni and wine; add the mussels and cook 3 minutes. Add the shrimp and reduce the heat. When the shrimp are firm and the mussels open, remove from heat.

Lay the sole fillets on a board and roll them up from the small end to the large end. Remove the shrimp and mussels from the pot; keep warm. Pass the cooking liquid through a fine sieve and return to pan. Add the vegetables to the stock and reheat. Add the rolled sole, the halibut and the cod. Then add the scallops and heat through, about 2 minutes, but do not overcook. Remove from heat and transfer fish and vegetables to a casserole. Add the shrimp and mussels and keep warm.

Return the liquid to the heat and reduce until it coats the back of a spoon. Remove from heat and whisk in softened butter, one piece at a time. Add chopped tarragon. Pour sauce over seafood. Makes 4 servings.

PEARS IN PUFF PASTRY WITH CREME ANGLAISE

4 Puff Pastry rectangles, about 3-by-5-inches each (8 ounces puff pastry dough) (page 149)
Pastry Cream (following)
Crème Anglaise (following)
4 Poached Pears, cored (page 54 and omit glaze)
Sugar

Place pastry in a baking pan and bake in a 425°F. oven for 8 minutes. Reduce temperature to 350°F. and bake 10 minutes longer or until cooked through. Prepare Pastry Cream, Crème Anglaise and Poached Pears. Cut pears in half and slice on a bias. Split pastry in half and cover the bottom with Pastry Cream. Arrange the sliced pears on the cream. Spoon Crème Anglaise on chilled plates. If desired, sprinkle sugar on the top piece of pastry and caramelize with a hot poker. Set top piece of pastry on the pears and place on pool of custard in the center of the plate. Serve warm. Makes 4 servings.

PASTRY CREAM In a saucepan beat 3 egg yolks until light and mix in ¼ cup sugar, 2 ½ tablespoons flour and 1 cup milk. Add 1 split vanilla bean. Cook, stirring constantly, over medium heat until thickened. Remove from heat and remove vanilla bean. Let cool.

CREME ANGLAISE Beat 3 egg yolks and 2 tablespoons sugar in a double boiler. Add 1 cup hot milk. Cook over hot water, stirring, until custard coats a spoon. Let cool. If desired, add 1 cup strawberry or raspberry puree as a tint just before serving.

Mary Sue Milliken
Susan Feniger
CITY CAFE
Los Angeles, California

Mary Sue Milliken, l., Susan Feniger, r.

A creative partnership, unique in the restaurant trade, works for a team of indefatigable young women chefs: Mary Sue Milliken, 26, and Susan Feniger, 30, part-owner, of the tiny eleven-table City Cafe restaurant in the revitalized Melrose Avenue area of Los Angeles.

Milliken, from St. Clair, Michigan, and Feniger, from Toledo, Ohio, abandoned promising college careers for the love of food. Both changed to professional culinary schools instead. Feniger enrolled at the Culinary Institute of America, in Hyde Park, New York, and Milliken, at Chicago's Washburne Trade School.

They met in the kitchen of the renowned Chicago restaurant, Le Perroquet, as the first women to enter owner Jovan Trebyovich's domain. "I wasn't deterred by Jovan's offering me a job as a hatcheck girl," says Milliken, "and my persistence finally paid off when I got a job in the kitchen a year later and was ecstatic when Susan arrived three months later." At Le Perroquet, their training in kitchen management meant perfection the first time around, which is indispensable to their present operation where space is at a premium.

Later, they lost touch as Feniger went to the elite Ma Maison in Los Angeles and Milliken's former employers at Let Them Eat Cake Bakery in Chicago enticed her to be chef at their Society Cafe in Deerfield, Illinois.

After some time, determined to enhance their knowledge of fine cuisines, both crossed the Atlantic within days of each other. Milliken worked in Paris at Le Restaurant d'Olympe and Feniger worked at L'Oasis on the French Riviera. They were thrilled when they accidentally found each other in Paris and vowed someday they would work together back in America.

Feniger arrived first, penniless, at the miniscule City Cafe two-and-a-half years ago and cooked on a hot plate in the twelve-by-thirteen-foot kitchen. Within three months she became part owner and three months later was joined by Milliken, who was eagerly awaiting an opportunity to reunite.

Space and equipment problems notwithstanding, they prepare seventeen desserts, smoke their own meat and other foods, produce herbed vinegars and marinated goat cheese, ship in coffee from San Francisco weekly as well as buy fish, meat, vegetables and fruits daily.

"Collaboration is the key," says Feniger. "It gives us relief when things get to be too much and motivation when things loosen up."

They also believe their "city cuisine" reflects their desire to stay on the move, to constantly change, to share what inspires and surprises them. This, they explain, "is what helps the staff stay active and makes dining at City Cafe so interesting."

AN AUTUMN DINNER

Fish Tartare

Marinated Sirloin with Gorgonzola

Roasted Potatoes

Corn on the Cob with Chili and Lime

Fresh Lemon Hazelnut Tart

FISH TARTARE

8 ounces salmon fillet, cut in ¼-inch cubes
8 ounces halibut fillet, cut in ¼-inch cubes
Juice of 2 limes
Salt and freshly ground black pepper to taste
1 egg yolk
1 tablespoon Dijon-style mustard
½ cup olive oil
½ cup cornichons, chopped
¼ cup capers, chopped
4 shallots, chopped
2 tablespoons chopped fresh parsley
1 tablespoon snipped fresh chives
Baguette slices for accompaniment

Sprinkle fish with lime juice, salt and pepper. Whisk egg yolk and mustard in a small bowl and whip in olive oil slowly. Stir in cornichons, capers, shallots, parsley and chives. Mix mayonnaise with fish and refrigerate. Serve chilled on small plates accompanied by baguette slices. Makes 4 servings.

MARINATED SIRLOIN WITH GORGONZOLA

1 cup olive oil
2 tablespoons dry mustard
2 garlic cloves, pureed
1 tablespoon Worcestershire sauce
1 teaspoon soy sauce
Dash Tabasco sauce
1 tablespoon fresh lemon juice
Salt and freshly ground black pepper to taste
1 piece beef sirloin (about 2 pounds), well-trimmed
Gorgonzola Sauce (following)

Reserve 2 tablespoons olive oil. In a bowl mix together the remaining olive oil, mustard, garlic, Worcestershire, soy, Tabasco, lemon juice and salt and pepper. Place meat in a plastic container, cover with marinade and refrigerate overnight, turning occasionally. Two hours before roasting let meat warm to room temperature.

In a large skillet heat the 2 tablespoons oil until hot and sear meat on both sides. Roast in a 375°F. oven until a meat thermometer registers 130°F., about 15 minutes. Remove meat from pan and reserve pan drippings for sauce. Slice meat in ½ -inch strips and accompany with Gorgonzola Sauce. Makes 4 servings.

GORGONZOLA SAUCE Scrape pan drippings into a saucepan and add 6 finely diced shallots. Sauté shallots about 5 minutes and add ⅔ cup Madeira. Reduce to one-half. Add 1 ½ cups Veal Stock (page 147) and reduce to 1 cup. Whip 4 tablespoons butter and 4 ounces Gorgonzola cheese, in pieces, into the sauce. Season with salt and freshly ground black pepper to taste.

ROASTED POTATOES

5 large baking potatoes
½ pound butter, clarified (page 146)
Salt and freshly ground black pepper to taste

Peel potatoes and slice very thinly with a mandoline or potato peeler. Wash in cold running water until the water runs clear and most of the starch has been rinsed off. Drain well and pat dry with a towel. In a bowl toss with clarified butter and season with salt and pepper. Lay potatoes on a sheet pan, patting them flat, so that they barely overlap. If necessary use two pans. Bake in a 450°F. oven for 25 to 30 minutes or until golden brown. Serve immediately. Makes 4 servings.

CORN ON THE COB WITH CHILI AND LIME

4 ears sweet corn
¼ pound butter
¾ teaspoon chili powder
3 tablespoons lime juice
Salt to taste

Husk corn and with a sharp knife slice each ear into 1-inch rounds. Cook corn in a large pot of boiling salted water just until tender, about 3 minutes. Meanwhile in a small saucepan melt butter with the chili powder. Stir in lime juice and salt to taste. Drain corn and toss with chili butter. Makes 4 servings.

FRESH LEMON HAZELNUT TART

2 lemons
1 ¾ cups hazelnuts
1 tablespoon all-purpose flour
3 eggs, separated
1 ½ cups sugar
3 egg whites
Confectioners' sugar

Grate the lemon peel. Peel, then separate the lemon into segments, removing seeds and white pith. Grind nuts in a food processor and reserve ¾ cup. Mix remaining nuts with flour. In a bowl beat egg yolks until pale in color and gradually beat in ¾ cup of the sugar. Mix in lemon peel and fold in the nut-flour mixture. Pour batter into a buttered, floured 9-inch cake pan. Bake in a 375°F. oven for 15 to 20 minutes or until the cake springs back when touched lightly. Cool on a rack 10 minutes. Remove cake from pan and arrange lemon segments on top and drizzle over any juice. Place on a baking sheet and prepare meringue.

Whip the 6 egg whites until foamy and gradually add the remaining ¾ cup sugar, beating until stiff shiny peaks form. Fold remaining ¾ cup ground nuts into the meringue and spread over the lemon segments, covering cake completely. Bake in a 350°F. oven 10 to 15 minutes, or until lightly browned. Serve warm, dusted with confectioners' sugar. Makes 8 servings.

A SUMMER DINNER

Salmon Mousse with
Watercress Mayonnaise

Soupe au Pistou

Roast Poussin
with Cilantro and Fresh
Tomato Sauce

Cracked Wheat

Limestone Lettuce with
House Dressing

Plum Tart

SALMON MOUSSE WITH WATERCRESS MAYONNAISE

1 ¼ pounds boneless, skinless
  salmon, cut in ½ -inch cubes
Salt and freshly ground black
  pepper to taste
3 cups Fish Stock (page 147) or
  clam juice
1 cup mushroom stems or
  sliced mushrooms
1 tablespoon unsalted butter
1 cup brandy
3 shallots, peeled and sliced
½ ounce unflavored gelatin
Pinch freshly grated nutmeg
Dash Tabasco sauce
1 cup whipping cream
Watercress Mayonnaise
  (following)

Season salmon with salt and
pepper and place in a large
sauté pan or casserole. Bring
fish stock to a boil and pour
over the fish. Cover with buttered waxed paper and bake in
a 375°F. oven for 8 to 10 minutes or until barely cooked
through. Strain liquid and
reserve.
    While still warm puree
salmon in a food processor or
blender. Set aside. Using the
same pan, sauté mushrooms in
butter until glazed. Deglaze
pan with brandy and reduce by
one-half. In a food processor or
blender, puree the shallots and
the reserved fish stock and add
to the brandy. Continue cooking until 1 cup liquid remains.
Strain, discarding mushrooms
and shallots. Sprinkle gelatin
over the warm stock and let
stand until dissolved. Place
pureed salmon in a bowl over
ice. Whip the warm gelatin
mixture into the salmon and
adjust seasoning with salt,
pepper, nutmeg and Tabasco.
Let cool. Whip cream until stiff
and fold in. Place in a glass loaf
pan and cover with plastic
wrap. Chill. Serve cut in slices
with Watercress Mayonnaise.
Makes 10 servings.

WATERCRESS MAYONNAISE
Wash 1 bunch watercress thoroughly. In a food processor or
blender puree the leaves only
with ½ cup sour cream, ½ teaspoon salt, and 1 teaspoon
fresh lemon juice. Stir in ¾ cup
mayonnaise and add a dash of
Tabasco sauce to taste. Chill.

SOUPE AU PISTOU

⅓ cup white beans, soaked
  overnight
3 quarts well-seasoned Chicken
  Stock (page 147)
2 small red potatoes, cut in ½ -
  inch dice
2 large carrots, cut in ½ -inch
  dice
1 large onion, cut in ½ -inch
  dice
¼ pound green beans, sliced
  diagonally
1 zucchini, cut in ½ -inch dice
1 yellow crookneck squash, cut
  in ½ -inch dice
2 tomatoes, peeled, seeded and
  cut in ½ -inch dice
Basil Sauce (following)
Salt and freshly ground black
  pepper to taste

In a large pot bring chicken
stock to a boil and skim off any
foam. Reduce flame, add beans
and simmer 15 minutes. Add
potatoes, carrots and onions
and cook 15 minutes longer.
Add green beans, zucchini,
yellow squash and tomatoes
and cook until all vegetables
are tender. Ladle into bowls
and dollop with Basil Sauce.
Makes 8 to 10 servings.

BASIL SAUCE Puree 3 peeled
garlic cloves in 2 tablespoons
olive oil in a blender or food
processor and slowly add the
leaves from 1 bunch basil until
pureed. Mix this puree with ¾
cup grated Gruyère cheese.

ROAST POUSSIN WITH CILANTRO AND FRESH TOMATO SAUCE

6 poussins (baby chickens)
Salt and freshly ground black
  pepper to taste
4 teaspoons turmeric
4 tablespoons olive oil
3 bunches cilantro, leaves only
Cracked wheat for
  accompaniment
Fresh Tomato Sauce (following)

Carefully bone each chicken
into two pieces removing all
bones except the wings and leg
bone, making 12 pieces or two
chicken halves per serving. Lay
out boned chickens, skin side
down; season well with salt

and pepper and brush with a
paste made from the turmeric
and 2 tablespoons olive oil. Lay
the cilantro leaves on the
chicken. Roll each piece, keeping the breast inside. Tie each
with three strings.
  In a skillet heat remaining oil
and sauté chicken rolls, turning to brown all sides. Roast in
a 400°F. oven for 10 minutes.
Transfer chicken to a hot platter
and remove strings. Reserve
pan juices for sauce. Serve
poussin on a bed of cracked
wheat and top with Fresh Tomato Sauce. Makes 6 servings.

FRESH TOMATO SAUCE In the
pan used to roast the poussin,
sauté 4 tablespoons finely
chopped shallots over medium
heat. Add 3 cups peeled,
seeded, diced tomatoes, 1 teaspoon fresh lemon juice and
salt and freshly ground pepper
to taste. Cook 3 to 5 minutes,
stirring. Whisk in 4 tablespoons butter, one piece at a
time; when blended add 3 tablespoons chopped fresh
parsley.

LIMESTONE LETTUCE WITH HOUSE DRESSING

6 heads limestone lettuce
2 tablespoons Tiparos fish
  sauce (imported from
  Thailand)*
1 tablespoon fresh lemon juice
1 tablespoon rice wine vinegar*
2 tablespoons vegetable oil
1 tablespoon soy sauce
1 tablespoon Pernod or other
  anise-flavored liqueur
2 tablespoons sesame oil*
2 teaspoons very finely
  chopped fresh ginger

Wash lettuce well and pat dry.
For dressing, mix together the
fish sauce, lemon juice, vinegar, oil, soy sauce, Pernod, sesame oil and ginger. Pour over
greens and toss lightly. Spoon
greens onto salad plates.
Makes 6 servings.

Available at Oriental markets.

PLUM TART

Pastry Shell for 10-inch tart pan
  with removable bottom,
  baked
¾ done (page 150)
½ cup sugar
½ cup blanched slivered
  almonds
6 tablespoons butter
1 egg yolk
1 egg
1 tablespoon rum
1 teaspoon vanilla extract
8 plums
Streusel Topping (following)
Whipped cream (optional)

Prepare Pastry Shell. For filling, process sugar and almonds in a food processor until finely ground. In a mixing
bowl beat butter until creamy
and mix in nut mixture. Add
egg yolk, egg, rum and vanilla
and mix just until blended.
Spread in partially baked pastry shell making an even layer
and bake in a 350°F. oven for 10
minutes. Halve plums and remove pits. Arrange halves skin
side up on the tart. Sprinkle
with Streusel Topping and
bake 15 to 20 minutes longer or
until plums are soft and the
crust is golden brown. Let cool
on a rack. If desired, accompany with whipped cream.
Makes 8 servings.

STREUSEL TOPPING In a mixing
bowl cream together ¼ cup
butter, ⅓ cup firmly packed
brown sugar and a pinch salt
and cinnamon. Add ¾ cup all-
purpose flour and mix just until crumbly.

Bill Neal
CROOK'S CORNER
Chapel Hill, North Carolina

"I've always liked the festivity of cooking," claims chef and co-owner Bill Neal, 33, of Crook's Corner, Chapel Hill, North Carolina. "It's a real giving thing, and your approach to food is indicative of your approach to life." When everything is going well at work, Neal says it's "just like Christmas!"

Neal describes Crook's Corner as "an American answer to a French bistro—like the middle-class gusto in French food." The black, white and chrome interior is a backdrop for a changing gallery of works by local artists. The bar features black and white tile; black formica tables with chrome bands contrast with the heavy white dinner china.

"It's a one-of-a-kind place, and I want it to be a great neighborhood restaurant," says Neal, who made it with no formal training.

A graduate of Duke University, Neal spent a frustrating year teaching. He left his job to return to graduate school. While his wife worked nights at a country club, Neal prepared dinner for himself and their year-and-a-half-old son. It was a chore that changed his life. He cooked his way through Julia Child and loved it.

After two years of catering and baking, he opened a French country restaurant, La Residence, with his wife in 1976. It was an instant success. When his marriage ended in 1982, Neal left La Residence. Still wanting a restaurant of his own, he changed direction and opened Crook's Corner in March, 1982, in a building that had variously functioned as a service station, taxi stand, vagrant refuge, bait-and-tackle shop and barbecue cafe. Now Neal's casual eatery, marked by a large pig planted on its roof, attracts a very respectable clientele to the once run-down area.

The blend of flavors of Neal's specialties encompasses barbecued spareribs and such Southern sweets as black bottom pie and banana pudding, sharing the spotlight with Italian, French, Oriental and vegetarian cuisines. Homespun dishes like meat loaf, stuffed cabbage rolls and hush puppies are available alongside more sophisticated dishes such as spinach pasta with scallops.

Neal likes the university atmosphere of Chapel Hill. He points out that the 1980 United States government census rated Chapel Hill the best-educated town in the country, with the highest percentage of Ph.D's. "There are big-city advantages here, but with a population of only 40,000," says Neal.

A SPRING DINNER

Garlic Soup with Mushrooms

Baked Artichokes with
Goat Cheese and Mustard
Vinaigrette

Fish in Creole Sauce

Fresh and Dried Fruit Plate

GARLIC SOUP WITH MUSHROOMS

1 small onion, chopped
2 tablespoons butter
6 cups Chicken Stock (page 147)
12 large garlic cloves, peeled
6 slices stale French bread
Salt and white pepper to taste
¾ cup whipping cream
1 ¼ cups sliced mushrooms
Finely chopped fresh parsley, chervil and chives for garnish

In a large saucepot sauté onion in 1 tablespoon of the butter until translucent. Add stock, garlic and bread. Cover and simmer for 30 minutes or until garlic is tender. Let cool slightly, then puree in a food processor or blender. Strain. Season with salt and pepper.

Add cream and reheat slowly. Meanwhile, in a skillet sauté mushrooms in the remaining 1 tablespoon butter over medium-high heat and stir into the soup. Ladle into bowls and garnish with chopped herbs. Makes 8 servings.

BAKED ARTICHOKES WITH GOAT CHEESE AND MUSTARD VINAIGRETTE

4 large artichokes
6 ounces goat cheese
1 tablespoon extra virgin olive oil
1 egg
1 garlic clove, minced
1 tablespoon fresh chopped basil or ¾ teaspoon dried basil
1 teaspoon fresh chopped rosemary or ¼ teaspoon dried rosemary
1 tablespoon fresh bread crumbs
Salt and freshly ground black pepper to taste
Olive oil and white wine for baking
Mustard Vinaigrette (following)

Trim artichokes, removing the outer leaves, cut off the stem and scoop out the choke. Cook in a large pot of boiling salted water, seasoned with 1 tablespoon oil and 1 teaspoon vinegar, until tender, about 30 to 35 minutes. Mix together the cheese, oil, egg, garlic, basil, rosemary, bread crumbs, salt and pepper. Divide the mixture into four portions and spoon in the center of each artichoke. Place artichokes in a deep pan and drizzle with olive oil and add enough white wine to cover the bottom of the pan. Cover and bake in a 375°F. oven for 25 to 35 minutes, or until the cheese mixture is just set. Uncover and chill.

Open the artichokes up like a flower to serve. Surround with the Mustard Vinaigrette. Drizzle a little sauce on the leaves as well. Makes 4 servings.

MUSTARD VINAIGRETTE In a saucepan stir together 2 tablespoons Dijon-style mustard, 2 tablespoons water and 1 tablespoon cider vinegar. Heat, stirring until steaming, but do not boil. Remove from heat and stir in ¼ cup olive oil. Let cool. Add 1 tablespoon chopped fresh parsley, chives and chervil.

FISH IN CREOLE SAUCE

1 ½ to 2 pounds firm, white
  fish such as swordfish, halibut
  or shark
Olive oil
Salt and freshly ground black
  pepper to taste
1 medium onion, slivered
1 each sweet red, green and
  yellow pepper, halved,
  seeded and julienned
¼ cup finely diced boiled ham
2 garlic cloves, minced
1 cup thinly sliced okra
2 tomatoes, peeled, seeded and
  diced
1 tablespoon chopped fresh
  basil or ¾ teaspoon dried basil
Dash Tabasco sauce

Brush fish with oil and sprinkle
with salt and pepper. Set aside
while preparing sauce. In a
large skillet sauté onion and
peppers in 2 tablespoons of oil
over medium heat. Add ham
and garlic and remove from
heat. In a separate pan sauté
okra in 1 tablespoon oil. Add
tomatoes and basil and mix
into the pepper mixture. Season with salt and pepper and a
dash of Tabasco.
   Grill fish over medium-hot
coals or broil, turning to grill
both sides, and cooking about
8 to 10 minutes or just until the
flesh barely separates along its
natural seams. Arrange fish on
a platter and spoon over the
sauce. Makes 4 servings.

FRESH AND DRIED
FRUIT PLATE

Arrange on a platter a selection
of fresh seasonal fruit, such as
pears, tangerines, grapes and
cherries; dried fruits such as
apricots, prunes, raisins and
dates; salted almonds and
pecans and bittersweet
chocolate such as pastilles.
Accompany with coffee,
brandy or champagne,
depending on the occasion.

A WINTER DINNER

Escarole Salad with
Mushrooms

Braised Pork Chops
with Baby Limas
and Whole Garlic

Pecan Shortbread

ESCAROLE SALAD WITH
MUSHROOMS

4 heads escarole
8 ounces medium-sized
  mushrooms
2 slices blanched bacon,
  chopped
2 tablespoons peanut oil
1 tomato, peeled, seeded and
  chopped
½ cup chopped green onions
6 tablespoons virgin olive oil
2 tablespoons rice wine
  vinegar*
Salt and freshly ground black
  pepper to taste

Remove all the outer leaves of
the escarole, leaving only the
light-colored centers. (Save dis-
cards for soup.) Arrange each
center on a salad plate. In a
large skillet over medium-high
heat sauté mushrooms and bacon in peanut oil, cooking until
tender. Immediately spoon
over the lettuce hearts. Mix together the tomato, onions, olive oil, vinegar and salt and
pepper and spoon over the top.
Makes 4 servings.

Available at Oriental markets.

45

BRAISED PORK CHOPS WITH BABY LIMAS AND WHOLE GARLIC

4 thick pork chops
1 tablespoon olive oil
1 onion, finely chopped
½ cup dry vermouth
1 ½ cups Beef Stock (page 147)
2 dozen unpeeled garlic cloves
1 tablespoon quick-mixing
  flour*
4 large sprigs thyme or 1
  teaspoon dried thyme
4 sprigs rosemary or 1
  teaspoon crumbled dried
  rosemary
1 package (10 ounces) frozen
  baby lima beans
Polenta for accompaniment

In a large skillet or flameproof casserole sauté pork chops in oil, turning to brown both sides. Transfer to a baking dish. Add onion to the skillet and cook until translucent. Add vermouth and reduce by half. Stir in stock and garlic. Blend in flour and cook until thickened. Add thyme and rosemary. Pour sauce mixture over the meat, cover, and bake in a 350°F. oven 1 hour. Blanch lima beans, add to the chops, cover and bake 20 minutes longer, or until the chops are tender. Serve accompanied with polenta, made with lots of freshly grated Parmesan cheese. Makes 4 servings.

Quick-mixing flour (sometimes called instant flour) incorporates readily in this sauce. Or use 1 tablespoon cornstarch blended with 1 tablespoon cold water.

PECAN SHORTBREAD

2 cups all-purpose flour
½ cup cornstarch
½ cup sugar
½ teaspoon salt
½ pound butter
½ teaspoon vanilla extract
2 egg yolks
2 teaspoons water
1 cup finely chopped pecans,
  walnuts or almonds

Into a bowl sift together the flour, cornstarch, sugar and salt. Cut in butter and mix in vanilla. Beat egg yolks with water and quickly stir in. Mix in nuts. Turn out dough on a lightly floured board and knead lightly and rapidly. Chill.

Roll out dough about ⅜ -inch thick. Cut into desired shapes and place on an ungreased cookie sheet. Bake in a 375°F. oven for 20 minutes or until golden brown. Let cool on a rack. Makes about 4 dozen.

NOTE For a variation, while cookies are slightly warm, dust tops with confectioners' sugar.

Philippe Jeanty
DOMAINE CHANDON
Yountville, California

Set amid gracious, sprawling oaks in the beautiful Napa Valley is the restaurant and winery, Domaine Chandon. Within the architecturally exciting, contemporary building, sheathed in glass and native stone and capped with arched wood ceilings, the dining room showcases the winery's own sparkling wines in light, elegant, nouvelle cuisine style.

Chef Philippe Jeanty, 27, is from the Champagne region of France. Starting at age fifteen, he served a three-year apprenticeship in the kitchen of chef Joseph Thuet at Moet and Chandon. Jeanty spent the obligatory two years in the French army, as a pastry chef, and attended the hotel and restaurant school in Reims.

For the opening festivities of Domaine Chandon in 1977, he traveled with his mentor, Thuet, to California. Jeanty stayed on, becoming head chef in just over a year. His kitchen at Domaine Chandon prepares

luncheon for an average of 280 guests and dinner for eighty or more nightly.

Appetizer specialties include fish soup in the style of southern France, squab salad with hazelnut dressing, fresh linguine with smoked salmon and caviar and lamb ravioli with Roquefort sauce. Entrées may encompass grilled yellowfin tuna with fresh herbs, salmon with champagne and sorrel, venison in cassis sauce and lamb noisettes with rosemary and balsamic vinegar. Desserts can be a pair of rolled lace wafers filled with praline and pistachio ice cream, an ethereal white and dark chocolate mousse cake and honey ice cream with blackberries and meringue.

A SPRING DINNER

Tomato Soup en Croute

Prawns in Champagne

Fresh Asparagus

Honey Ice Cream with Berries

TOMATO SOUP EN CROUTE

2 medium onions, peeled and chopped
2 tablespoons unsalted butter
2 pounds tomatoes, peeled, seeded and quartered
4 garlic cloves, peeled
1 bay leaf
Pinch thyme
Salt and white pepper to taste
2 cups whipping cream
1 package (17 ounces) frozen puff pastry, thawed
¼ cup julienned carrots, julienned leeks and green onion rings for garnish
Egg wash (1 egg yolk beaten with 1 tablespoon water)

In a large saucepot cook onions in butter until soft. Add tomatoes, garlic, bay leaf, thyme, salt and pepper and cook slowly, uncovered for 1 ½ hours. Puree in a blender or food processor and strain. Stir in cream and correct the seasoning. Chill.

Roll out the puff pastry about ⅛-inch thick. Cut circles of pastry about 2 inches larger in diameter than the ovenproof soup bowls in which the soup will be served. Ladle the cool soup into the bowls and garnish with a spoonful of the julienned carrots and leeks and onion rings. Paint the surface of the pastry with an egg wash and lay a circle of pastry on top of the bowl, egg wash side down and press to seal to the sides of the bowl. Refrigerate for 1 hour or longer to set the pastry. Brush top of the pastry with egg wash and bake in a 450°F. oven for 15 to 20 minutes or until the pastry is puffed and golden brown. Makes 6 servings.

PRAWNS IN CHAMPAGNE

3 shallots, chopped
6 tablespoons unsalted butter
1 ½ cups brut champagne
1 fennel bulb, thinly sliced
1 carrot, julienned
1 leek, julienned
Salt and white pepper to taste
36 medium-sized raw prawns, peeled and deveined (shells reserved)
1 sprig chervil or tarragon

Sauté the shallots in 2 teaspoons butter in a saucepan. Add champagne and shells from the prawns and cook for 15 minutes on medium heat. Strain and reduce by half. In a small skillet sauté the fennel, carrot and leek in 2 teaspoons butter and season with salt and pepper. Put this garnish on warm plates. Place prawns in a saucepan with the stock and simmer for 3 to 4 minutes. Lift prawns out of stock with a slotted spoon and arrange on the center of the plates. Reduce cooking liquid by half and whisk in remaining butter, one piece at a time, mixing constantly. Add salt and pepper to taste. Spoon sauce over prawns and garnish with chervil or tarragon leaves. Makes 6 servings.

HONEY ICE CREAM WITH BERRIES

12 egg yolks
1 cup honey
2 ¼ cups whole milk
2 ¼ cups whipping cream
Berries for garnish:
   strawberries, blackberries or
   blueberries
Mint sprigs for garnish

Beat egg yolks until thick and light in color and beat in honey. Scald milk and pour into the honey-yolk mixture. Turn into a double boiler and cook over hot water, stirring constantly, until the custard coats a spoon. Place pan in a bowl of ice water and cool, stirring. Blend in cream. Chill. Churn in an ice cream freezer following manufacturer's instructions until frozen. Serve in bowls topped by a cluster of berries and a sprig of mint. Makes 8 to 10 servings.

AN AUTUMN DINNER

Linguine with Truffles

Chicken with Morels

Buttered Sugar Snap Peas

Frozen Coffee Mousse

LINGUINE WITH TRUFFLES

1 ¾ to 2 cups all-purpose flour
2 eggs
Pinch salt
2 tablespoons olive oil

2 fresh black or white truffles (medium)*
1 ½ teaspoons unsalted butter
1 shallot, chopped
½ cup whipping cream
2 egg yolks, lightly beaten
Salt and white pepper to taste
Chervil for garnish (optional)

Prepare pasta by mixing flour, eggs, salt and 1 tablespoon oil, according to a standard pasta method (page 148). Roll out and cut into linguine. Cook pasta in a large amount of boiling salted water with 1 tablespoon olive oil until just tender, about 2 minutes. Drain and cool under cold water. Do in advance, if desired.

Chop one of the truffles. Melt butter in a saucepan and add shallot and sauté for 1 minute. Add cream and reduce for 2 minutes. Add pasta and heat until hot through. Mix in the chopped truffle and egg yolks. Season with salt and pepper and spoon onto hot plates. Garnish with chervil, if desired. Using a truffle grater, slice the other truffle onto the pasta in front of guests. Makes 4 servings.

*Available at gourmet markets.

CHICKEN WITH MORELS

8 dried morel mushrooms
1 chicken, quartered (about
2 ¼ pounds)
2 tablespoons each butter and
  vegetable oil
2 shallots, minced
⅔ cup brut champagne or dry
  white wine
1 cup whipping cream
Salt and white pepper to taste

Reconstitute the morels in a bowl of water for 1 hour, rinsing 5 or 6 times to remove all dirt.

In a large skillet sauté chicken in butter and oil for 10 minutes or until golden brown. Add the shallots and cook until soft but not brown and the chicken is almost tender, about 10 minutes longer. Deglaze the chicken and shallots with the champagne or wine, add the morels and cream and bring to a boil. Cook for about 2 minutes, remove chicken to a hot platter or individual plates and reduce the sauce until thickened. Season with salt and pepper to taste. Serve the chicken napped with sauce. Makes 2 generous servings.

FROZEN COFFEE MOUSSE

4 tablespoons instant coffee
  powder
4 tablespoons cold water
4 eggs, separated
⅔ cup sugar
2 egg whites
2 cups whipping cream
Cocoa powder or fresh fruit for
  garnish

Dissolve coffee powder in water. Beat egg yolks and sugar in the top of a double boiler over hot water, whipping until mixture reaches a light, creamy consistency. Stir in coffee and let cool. Whip the 6 egg whites until stiff, but not dry. Whip cream until stiff. Fold the beaten egg whites into the yolk mixture. Gently fold in the whipped cream. Turn into a 1 ½ -quart mold, lined with a foil collar, or individual molds. Freeze until firm, about 4 to 5 hours. Spoon from the large mold into dessert bowls or unmold individual servings onto dessert plates. Garnish with a light dusting of cocoa, if desired, or with diced fresh fruit. Makes 6 to 8 servings.

Stanley Eichelbaum
EICHELBAUM & CO.
San Francisco, California

Former drama critic Stanley Eichelbaum switched careers a few years ago, enrolled in the California Culinary Academy, and then opened a charming takeout food store and cafe in San Francisco.

"The thing that has always excited me is to get reviewed yourself," says Eichelbaum. "I find it an exhilarating and rewarding experience." He describes his current vocation as more vibrant and creative than his experience as a journalist.

At Eichelbaum & Co. elegant box lunches in four menu patterns—a pâté, chicken salad, a sandwich and quiche—are the shop's "bread and butter," according to Eichelbaum. Breakfast, lunch and dinner are also available to eat at the cafe.

A blackboard lists the specialties that change weekly. Creative salads include poached salmon and white beans in lemon-zested mayonnaise, slivered warm duck tossed with red and green peppers and homemade pasta, and mixed seafood in a brown rice pyramid.

Luncheon entrées include salmon and scallops with lemon tarragon sauce, strip steak with red wine sauce and chicken Françoise. Desserts produced at the cafe encompass a gorgeous chocolate bombe ringed with raspberries and showered with pistachios,

decorative individual fruit or almond tarts, apricot cheesecake, chocolate walnut tart or double chocolate brownies.

The limited and refined dinner menu presents fresh California cuisine that varies weekly. A typical summer menu offers a trio of first courses: leek and pistachio soup, tomato fettuccine with pesto sauce and roast veal salad with greens, grapes and green peppercorns.

A SUMMER DINNER

Fruit and Yogurt Gazpacho

Ballotine of Chicken with Wild Rice and Hazelnut Stuffing

Petite Green Beans with Tarragon

Lemon Cream Pistachio Tarts

FRUIT AND YOGURT
GAZPACHO

2 cucumbers, peeled, halved and seeded
2 garlic cloves, peeled
1 quart plain yogurt
3 tablespoons honey
1 pound Thompson seedless grapes
1 pound plums or red-skinned apples, diced
⅓ cup whipping cream
2 tablespoons toasted sliced almonds

In a food processor puree 1 cucumber with garlic, yogurt and honey and half the grapes. Chill. To serve, ladle into bowls and garnish with remaining cucumber, cut in dice, diced plums or apples (or both) and remaining grapes, cut in half. Drizzle cream over the fruit and sprinkle with toasted almonds. Makes 6 to 8 servings.

BALLOTINE OF CHICKEN
WITH WILD RICE
AND HAZELNUT
STUFFING*

1 chicken (3 ½ to 4 pounds)
1 tablespoon each olive oil and butter
1 medium onion, minced
3 stalks celery, finely chopped
½ cup mushrooms, finely chopped
2 garlic cloves, minced
½ pound (about 1 cup) ground pork
⅓ cup chicken fat, rendered, or butter
⅔ cup wild rice, cooked
2 eggs
⅓ cup hazelnuts, toasted and chopped
Salt and freshly ground black pepper to taste
Butter

Debone chicken by slitting down the back and working deftly and carefully with a boning knife to loosen the bones and rib cage. Pull out all bones including leg and wing bones until what's left is a chicken "that's like an old-fashioned suit of underwear." Try not to puncture the skin.

In a large skillet heat oil and butter over medium heat and sauté onion a few minutes. Add celery, mushrooms and garlic and sauté over low heat for 10 to 15 minutes. Add ground pork and cook 10 minutes longer. Place mixture in a bowl with chopped chicken fat or pieces of butter. Add cooked wild rice, eggs and chopped hazelnuts and mix lightly. Season with salt and pepper.

Lay chicken, skin down, on a chopping board. Spread stuffing on the chicken and stuff it in the leg cavities. Fold ends over and secure seams with wooden or metal skewers. Place seam side down on a rack in a roasting pan. Season with salt and pepper and dot with butter.

Roast in a 350°F. oven 1 hour or until skin is golden brown and a meat thermometer registers 150°F. Remove from the oven and let rest 10 to 15 minutes before serving. Slice in half and slice crosswise. Makes 6 to 8 servings.

Ballotine is a French term for a boned fowl, meat or fish that is stuffed, rolled, cooked and served hot.

LEMON CREAM PISTACHIO TARTS

Fluted Pastry Shells (page 20)
3 eggs
1 cup sugar
⅔ cup fresh lemon juice
1 tablespoon grated lemon peel
¼ pound butter, cut in pieces
Red currant jelly or melted
  chocolate
1 ½ cups whipping cream
Kirsch (optional)
Chopped pistachio nuts for
  garnish
Lemon twists for garnish

Prepare Fluted Pastry Shells. In a double boiler beat eggs until light; beat in sugar, lemon juice and lemon peel. Add butter, one piece at a time. Place over hot water and cook, stirring, until thickened. Cool. To assemble tarts, paint the bottom of the tart shells with melted red currant jelly or melted chocolate.

Whip cream until stiff and flavor with a dash of kirsch, if desired. Fold half of the cream into the lemon curd. Fill shells two-thirds full. Pipe a decorative border of the remaining whipped cream around the filled tarts and sprinkle centers with pistachios. Garnish with a twisted lemon slice. Makes 8 tarts.

AN AUTUMN DINNER

Mushroom Soup Deluxe

Braised Pork Loin Stuffed with Prunes and Apricots, served with Blueberry Sauce

Chocolate Truffle Cake

MUSHROOM SOUP DELUXE

½ cup dried mushrooms (porcini or shiitake)
1 tablespoon each olive oil and butter
1 large onion, chopped
2 leeks, chopped (white part only)
3 garlic cloves, minced
1 pound domestic mushrooms, sliced
3 tablespoons all-purpose flour
3 tablespoons tomato paste
1 quart Chicken Stock (page 147)
Salt and freshly ground black pepper to taste
½ cup sweet vermouth or sweet sherry
⅓ cup freshly grated Parmesan cheese
2 tablespoons chopped fresh parsley

Soak dried mushrooms in water to cover for 15 minutes. In a large soup pot heat oil and butter over low heat. Sauté onion, leeks and garlic until tender without browning. Remove mushrooms and reserve liquid. Discard hard stems of the mushrooms. Slice caps. Add both mushrooms to the soup pot and stir well. Sprinkle with flour, let cook 2 minutes, and stir in tomato paste. Add chicken stock. Cover and simmer 30 minutes. Season with salt and pepper to taste. Add vermouth or sherry and cook 10 minutes longer. Serve with a garnish of Parmesan cheese and chopped parsley. Makes 6 to 8 servings.

BRAISED PORK LOIN STUFFED WITH PRUNES AND APRICOTS, SERVED WITH BLUEBERRY SAUCE

1 center-cut pork loin (3 pounds)
4 ounces dried prunes
4 ounces dried apricots
1 to 2 tablespoons olive oil
1 medium onion, sliced
1 large carrot, sliced
3 stalks celery, sliced
3 garlic cloves, minced
1 cup white or red wine or port
2 cups Veal or Beef Stock (page 147)
1 teaspoon each fresh thyme and rosemary or ¼ teaspoon dried thyme and rosemary
1 bay leaf
4 parsley sprigs
Salt and freshly ground black pepper to taste
1 tablespoon cornstarch dissolved in 2 tablespoons wine
1 cup fresh or frozen blueberries, (thawed, if frozen)
Pinch of sugar (optional)

Slit loin partially along the bones and insert prunes and apricots in an alternate pattern in a straight line. Push slit together and tie loin securely with circles of string, starting at the center and working toward both ends.

In a Dutch oven heat oil over medium-high heat and brown loin on all sides, allowing about 10 minutes. Add onion, carrot, celery and garlic to oil and sauté until lightly browned. Deglaze with wine. Add stock, thyme, rosemary, bay leaf and parsley sprigs. Season meat with salt and pepper. Bring to a boil on top of the stove.

Cover and place in a 350°F. oven for 45 to 60 minutes or until the internal temperature of the pork is 150°F. Remove pork from the casserole and let stand on a warm platter.

Strain and degrease sauce. Reduce sauce by one-third to one-half. Stir in cornstarch paste and cook until thickened, about 2 minutes. Add blueberries and heat through. Taste and correct seasoning with salt, pepper, and pinch of sugar, if desired. Slice pork and serve with sauce over or under it. Makes 6 servings.

CHOCOLATE TRUFFLE CAKE

4 ounces semisweet chocolate
¼ pound unsalted butter
4 eggs, separated
2 tablespoons dark rum
¼ cup raspberry jam
3 tablespoons fresh lemon juice
Whipped cream (optional)
Chocolate shavings (optional)

In a double boiler melt chocolate and butter over hot water. Remove from heat and mix in lightly beaten egg yolks and rum. Transfer to a large bowl. Beat egg whites until stiff peaks form and fold into chocolate mixture just until blended. Butter and flour the bottom and sides of a 9-inch cake pan. Pour in cake batter. Bake in a 375°F. oven for 15 to 18 minutes or until cake is dry to the touch.

Let cool on a rack, then remove from pan. Heat raspberry jam and lemon juice in a small saucepan until bubbling. Strain over top center of cake and spread to the edges. Decorate top of cake with swirls of whipped cream if desired, and with chocolate shavings. Makes 8 servings.

Mark Miller
FOURTH STREET GRILL
Berkeley, California

The changing menu of the Fourth Street Grill in Berkeley evokes the flavors of the Caribbean and the Yucatan. "That food has my heart," says chef-owner Mark Miller, 35. Renowned for his eclectic list of specialties, Miller also takes from Mediterranean and Southeast Asian cuisines, all expressed in a fresh, unfussy California style.

Miller hates "prissy food," and insists it has got to have strong, pronounced flavors. "I don't tame anything down, and I avoid dairy products— cream and butter—and salt."

Mesquite-grilled meats, fresh pastas changing daily, herb-strewn salads and freshly churned sorbets are some of his trademarks. The restaurant makes its own chutneys, salsas, pickles, bread, sausages and pastries.

Seasonal specialties include carpaccio with virgin olive oil and Parmigiano-Reggiana cheese, Greek salad, steak tartare, fresh California mozzarella salad with tomatoes and herbs, Yucatan white sausage (housemade sausage with chicken, pork, fresh chilies and coriander), Louisiana hot sausage served with spiced applesauce, and paillard of top sirloin with salsa verde.

Miller studied Chinese history and anthropology as an undergraduate at the University of California, Berkeley, and did graduate work in anthropology. He then worked for Williams-Sonoma, an upscale kitchenware and specialty shop in San Francisco, for a year-and-a-half, and wrote a private newsletter, "The Market Basket," aimed at the serious cook, as well. He traveled to France several times a year and "took lots of cooking classes."

He joined Alice Waters and Jean Pierre Moulé in the kitchen of Chez Panisse in January, 1975, and experienced preparing four hundred or so new dishes yearly. He left in November, 1979 to open the Fourth Street Grill.

Since then travels to Mexico, Central America, the Caribbean and France, particularly Paris and Provence, have inspired many new recipes for his restaurant's menu. A two-week stay with food writer Richard Olney at his home in Provence was particularly exciting. "He is the best cook I have ever met," claims Miller.

The tables in Miller's starkly furnished, high-ceilinged restaurant are left bare for lunch and draped with pink cloths for dinner. A focal point of the room is a long bar where customers waiting for a table can purchase glasses of wine. Unidentified from the street, the restaurant's only marker is its address: 1820 Fourth Street.

A WINTER MENU

A WINTER MENU

Raw Artichoke Salad

Pasta with Lamb and
Chanterelles

Olive Oil, Rosemary and
Garlic Bread

Chocolate Prune Calvados
Torte

RAW ARTICHOKE SALAD

12 baby artichoke hearts
1 bulb fresh fennel
½ cup virgin olive oil
Juice of 1 lemon
Salt and freshly ground black
  pepper to taste
¼ pound Parmigiano-Reggiana
  cheese

Peel off the artichoke leaves until only the pale yellow centers
show. Slice thinly lengthwise
(using a non-carbon knife).
Slice fennel thinly. Arrange on
salad plates. Mix together the
oil, lemon juice and salt and
pepper and drizzle over. Using
a vegetable peeler, shave the
cheese over all. Serve at once.
Pass a pitcher of olive oil at the
table, if desired. Makes 4
servings.

PASTA WITH LAMB AND CHANTERELLES

4 tomatoes, quartered
  (optional)
1 pound raw boneless leg of
  lamb
⅔ cup virgin olive oil
Chopped fresh herbs:
  approximately 4 tablespoons
  oregano, 2 teaspoons
  rosemary and 1 ½ tablespoons
  thyme
1 medium red onion, diced

1 ½ pounds chanterelles,
  cleaned and sliced or
  domestic mushrooms, sliced
Salt and freshly ground black
  pepper to taste
½ cup dry red wine such as
  pinot noir, burgundy or light
  cabernet
2 to 3 cups Lamb or Veal Stock,
  flavored with dried cèpes
  (page 147)
1 tablespoon diced fresh garlic
1 pound fresh tagliarini or
  fettuccine
4 tablespoons unsalted butter

Place the tomatoes in a baking
pan and roast in a 450°F. oven
for 40 minutes, if desired. Slice
the lamb and cut into uniform

strips about ½-inch wide, 2 inches long and ¼-inch thick. Marinate in about ½ cup olive oil with half the herbs.

In a very large sauté pan sauté onion in remaining oil for 1 to 2 minutes. Add chanterelles and salt and pepper and sauté 3 to 4 minutes. Add wine and reduce by half. Add the stock, garlic, the tomatoes (if included), and about 1 tablespoon herbs. Cook until the stock is reduced by half.

Meanwhile, cook pasta in a large pot of boiling salted water until just tender. Drain and rinse under cold water. Add lamb to the sauce, heat through, about 1 minute, and whisk in butter, one tablespoon at a time, to finish sauce. Toss drained pasta in the sauce just to coat. Arrange on hot plates. Garnish with remaining chopped fresh herbs. Makes 4 servings.

OLIVE OIL, ROSEMARY AND GARLIC BREAD

2 tablespoons active dry yeast
2 ¼ cups warm water
1 teaspoon sugar
6 cups all-purpose flour
  (approximately)
⅔ cup whole wheat flour
1 tablespoon salt
⅔ cup virgin olive oil
1 tablespoon rosemary leaves
Cornmeal
Herb Topping (following)
Olive oil

Sprinkle yeast into ½ cup water, add sugar, and let stand until proofed. In a large mixing bowl place half the all-purpose flour, the whole wheat flour and the salt. Add remaining water and oil and mix well. Mix in proofed yeast and rosemary. Stir in remaining flour to make a soft dough. Knead until smooth and satiny. Cover and let rise until double in size. Shape into 2 round loaves and place on a baking pan sprinkled with cornmeal.

Prepare Herb Topping. With a finger poke random holes in the top of the loaves and fill with the Herb Topping. Cover and let rise until doubled. Brush with olive oil. Bake in a 375°F. oven for 40 minutes or until golden brown and loaves sound hollow when thumped. Makes 2 loaves.

HERB TOPPING Mix together 3 tablespoons butter, 1 tablespoon olive oil, 4 sliced roasted garlic cloves and 2 tablespoons fresh rosemary leaves.

CHOCOLATE PRUNE CALVADOS TORTE

½ cup pitted chopped prunes
⅓ cup mixed Calvados and
  Armagnac or brandy
9 ounces semisweet chocolate
⅓ cup espresso
6 ounces unsalted butter,
  softened
4 extra large eggs, separated
¾ cup plus 3 tablespoons sugar
½ cup cornstarch
¾ cup ground toasted pecans
⅛ teaspoon salt
Whipped cream flavored with
  Calvados

Marinate prunes in a mixture of Calvados and Armagnac while preparing torte. Melt chocolate with espresso in a double boiler over hot water, stirring until blended. Remove from heat and let cool slightly. Stir in butter. Transfer to a mixing bowl. Add egg yolks, one at a time, and beat in ¾ cup of the sugar until mixture is thick and light brown in color. Stir in cornstarch and pecans. Beat egg whites with salt until soft peaks form and gradually beat in the remaining 3 tablespoons sugar. Fold one-third of the whites into the batter. Gently fold in remaining whites. Turn into a buttered and floured 10-inch springform pan. Bake in a 350°F. oven for 35 to 40 minutes or until set. Let cool. Serve with whipped cream flavored with Calvados. Makes 10 to 12 servings.

A SPRING MENU

Ruby Red Grapefruit and
Avocado Salad

Tropical Fish Stew

Mexican Chocolate Ice Cream

RUBY RED GRAPEFRUIT AND AVOCADO SALAD

3 ruby red grapefruit
2 large Haas avocados
¼ cup grapefruit juice
¼ cup fruity Italian virgin olive
  oil
1 bunch cilantro for garnish

Peel and section grapefruit, discarding all white membrane, and reserving any grapefruit juice for dressing. Peel avocados and slice about ¾ -inch thick. On large, 12-inch dinner plates arrange avocado slices in a pinwheel pattern. Fill in with grapefruit sections making an asymmetrical pattern. Mix together the grapefruit juice and olive oil and drizzle over. Garnish with sprigs of cilantro. Makes 4 servings.

TROPICAL FISH STEW

½ cup virgin olive oil
1 red onion, chopped
3 large garlic cloves, minced
1 sweet red pepper, seeded
  and chopped
1 bunch cilantro
1 quart Fish Stock (page 147)
1 large tomato, diced
Juice of 2 limes and zest of 1
  lime
4 large fresh Monterey prawns
2 pounds diced fish fillets:
  barracuda and cod
⅔ cup diced fresh pineapple
1 each red and green jalapeño
  pepper, sliced
8 New Zealand cockles or small
  clams
4 squid, sliced
Fresh lime slices and cilantro
  sprigs for garnish
Dark rum or fresh pineapple
  juice (optional)

In a large skillet, heat oil and
sauté onion, garlic and pepper
over low heat, 10 minutes.
Place ½ bunch of cilantro in a
pan with the fish stock and let
simmer 10 to 15 minutes. Pour
stock into the sautéed vegetables and add tomato, lime juice
and zest, prawns, fish fillets,
pineapple, jalapeños and cockles. Bring to a boil, add squid
and remove from heat. Ladle
into bowls and garnish with
lime slices and cilantro sprigs.
If desired, lace the broth with a
dash of dark rum or sweeten it
with fresh pineapple juice.
Makes 4 to 6 servings.

MEXICAN CHOCOLATE
ICE CREAM

2 cups whole milk
1 split vanilla bean
8 egg yolks
1 cup sugar
¾ pound semisweet chocolate
¼ teaspoon cinnamon
⅓ cup ground toasted almonds
2 cups whipping cream

Scald milk with split vanilla
bean in a double boiler over hot
water. Beat egg yolks and
sugar until light and fluffy; stir
in part of the milk. Return to
the double boiler and cook over
hot water until custard coats a
spoon. Remove from heat, let
cool lightly and stir in chocolate and cinnamon. Place over a
pan of ice and let cool completely, stirring. Remove vanilla bean. Stir in almonds and
cream and chill. Churn in an
ice cream freezer following
manufacturer's instructions until frozen. Makes about 1 ½
quarts or 8 servings.

NOTE If desired, substitute 1
pound Mexican Ibarra chocolate (available at Latino markets) for the semisweet chocolate, sugar, cinnamon and
almonds.

Robert Kinkead
THE HARVEST
Cambridge, Massachusetts

Robert Kinkead, 30, chef of The Harvest in Cambridge, Massachusetts, describes the current approach to cooking in this country as one of energy and creativity. "American chefs are coming up with some great taste combinations," Kinkead believes, and "when all the experimentation goes away, I think we'll see a lot of exciting food in America."

"The new American cuisine is like its people—the cultural influences play off one another," says Kinkead. "The fare at The Harvest is a melting pot of all cuisines, done mostly with American products."

"I try to utilize taste combinations indigenous to the area and the thrust is geared to local products—pheasant, geese, wild mushrooms, wild berries and beach plums, lobster, sea bass, scallops and maple products," Kinkead explains.

The regional dishes at The Harvest reflect the seasons. In tandem with the menu, which changes daily, the wallcoverings vary as well, with tapestries and draperies in reds and oranges in autumn, grays and golds in winter and golds and greens in summer.

Inspired to be a chef by his father, "who dabbled with the pots and pans," Kinkead worked summers as a teenager at the County Fair on Cape Cod in Dennis, Massachusetts. By the time he left at age eighteen, he had progressed from washing dishes to cooking most of the family-style dinners of pot roast, fried chicken and seafood.

At the University of Massachusetts at Amherst, he received a B.A. in psychology, all the while working part-time as a chef.

Following graduation, he held a variety of cooking jobs that paid well, including chef at a pancake house, but weren't at the level he wanted to achieve. Determined to make food his career, he opted for quality experience over high salary. As sous chef at Joseph's in Boston and at Chillingsworth in Brewster, Kinkead received solid training in fine cuisine. He then accepted his present position at The Harvest.

At The Harvest, an outdoor terrace seats fifty-five in warm months. Indoors, the cafe and bar and main dining room provide 170 seats.

The dining room offers turkey and vegetable terrine with roasted pepper coulis; jalapeño tagliatelle with goose confit, sun-dried tomatoes, baby artichoke hearts and shiitakes; and oyster and lobster stew with vegetables and saffron.

Entrées include baked red snapper in parchment with scallops and mussels; sautéed smoked breast of duck with pears, pearl onions and collard greens; sautéed softshell crabs with corn masa and macadamia-cucumber-lime relish; and grilled breast of chicken with shrimp, garlic, feta, oregano and mushrooms.

A SUMMER DINNER

Lime-cured Salmon with Tomato Sorbet

Ravioli of Wild Mushrooms and Sweetbreads

Blueberry Chèvre Tart

LIME-CURED SALMON WITH TOMATO SORBET

6 very ripe tomatoes, peeled, pureed and strained
2 tablespoons balsamic vinegar
2 tablespoons vodka
Salt and freshly ground black pepper to taste
10 ounces trimmed Eastern or Norwegian salmon
Juice of 3 limes
Freshly cracked pepper and freshly cracked coriander seeds
Extra virgin olive oil
½ cup cilantro leaves

Place tomato puree in a saucepan and reduce by one-third. Stir in vinegar, vodka and salt and pepper. Churn in an ice cream freezer following manufacturer's instructions until frozen or freeze in ice cube trays until half frozen, beat until fluffy in a food processor, and return to the freezer and freeze until solid.

Slice salmon very thin and arrange 2 or 3 slices on individual plates. Paint with lime juice and let sit 15 minutes. Sprinkle with freshly cracked pepper and coriander seeds. Drizzle lightly with oil. Garnish generously with cilantro leaves. Place a scoop of sorbet alongside. Makes 4 servings.

RAVIOLI OF WILD MUSHROOMS AND SWEETBREADS

1 large shallot, chopped
¼ pound butter
¼ pound domestic mushrooms, coarsely chopped
½ pound assorted wild mushrooms, coarsely chopped or domestic mushrooms*
1 cup dried mushrooms, plumped in water and chopped (morels and cèpes)
½ cup Madeira
1 cup whipping cream
1 cup rich Veal Stock (page 147)
1 garlic clove, chopped
Salt and freshly ground black pepper to taste
⅛ teaspoon nutmeg
8 ounces natural cream cheese, softened
¾ pound Sweetbreads, soaked, blanched, cleaned and separated into nuggets (page 148)
1 teaspoon chopped fresh parsley
½ pound Pasta Dough (page 148)
Egg wash (1 egg beaten with 1 tablespoon water)
Semolina
Sweetbread Sauce (following)
Freshly grated Parmesan cheese

In a skillet sauté shallot in 1 tablespoon of the butter. Add fresh and dried mushrooms and sauté until the mushrooms are glazed. Add Madeira, cream, stock, garlic, salt and pepper and nutmeg and cook down until the sauce thickens.

Finely chop the sweetbreads and reserve one-third for the sauce. Add the remainder to the mushroom mixture. Mix in cream cheese. Cool. Roll out pasta dough thinly. With a ravioli cutter mark individual ravioli. Place a small spoonful of stuffing on each marked circle or square. Coat with egg wash and place a second sheet on top of the first. Press together. Cut out ravioli.

Place on a baking pan and sprinkle with a little semolina.

Cook in boiling salted water until tender, about 6 to 8 minutes. Serve napped with Sweetbread Sauce and topped with freshly grated Parmesan cheese. Makes 6 to 8 servings.

SWEETBREAD SAUCE In a large saucepan reduce ½ cup whipping cream, 1 ½ cups Veal Stock (page 147) and ¼ cup Madeira until thickened. Whisk in ¼ pound butter, one tablespoon at a time. Slice ¼ pound mushrooms and sauté in 1 tablespoon butter and mix in. Add the reserved diced sweetbreads.

Wild mushrooms are available at specialty produce markets.

BLUEBERRY CHEVRE TART

9-inch partially baked Tart Shell (page 150)
1 pound chèvre (such as Montrachet) or natural cream cheese
¾ cup sugar
3 eggs
½ teaspoon grated lemon peel
1 teaspoon vanilla extract
1 ½ cups blueberries
Apricot Blueberry Glaze (following)

Prepare tart shell. For filling, in a mixing bowl beat the chèvre or cream cheese until creamy and beat in the sugar. Add eggs, one at a time, and beat until smooth. Stir in lemon peel and vanilla. Spread in tart shell. Bake in a 350°F. oven for 20 minutes or just until set. Let cool. Cover top with blueberries and drizzle over with Apricot Blueberry Glaze. Makes 8 to 10 servings.

APRICOT BLUEBERRY GLAZE In a saucepan combine 1 cup blueberries, ½ cup apricot jelly and 1 tablespoon sugar. Bring to a simmer and cook until berries are mushy, about 6 minutes. Puree in a blender or food processor and strain through a sieve.

A LATE SUMMER DINNER

Succotash Soup
with Jonny Cakes

Lobster with Gold
Chanterelles

Berry Plate with
Double Cream

SUCCOTASH SOUP
WITH JONNY CAKES

3 ounces salt pork, diced
3 strips bacon, diced
1 small onion, diced
1 ½ quarts Chicken Stock (page 147)
2 pounds fresh shell beans (cranberry beans)
Salt and freshly ground black pepper to taste
2 bay leaves
4 ears corn, kernels cut from the cob
Jonny Cakes (following)
Crème Fraîche (page 146)

In a large soup pot sauté salt pork and bacon until almost crispy; reserve 1 tablespoon drippings for Jonny Cakes.

Add onion and cook until translucent. Add stock, beans, salt, pepper and bay leaves. Cover and simmer for 30 minutes or until beans start to soften. Add corn and cook uncovered, until a fairly thick consistency, about 10 minutes. For each serving, accompany with 3 half-dollar-sized Jonny Cakes and crème fraîche. Season with freshly ground pepper at the table.

JONNY CAKES In a bowl mix together ⅔ cup white cornmeal and 3 tablespoons all-purpose flour. Stir in 1 beaten egg, ⅔ cup milk, 1 ½ tablespoons melted butter, ¼ teaspoon salt and ¼ teaspoon sugar. Heat 1 tablespoon bacon drippings (reserved from Succotash Soup) in a large skillet. Drop teaspoons of batter into the pan and cook, turning to brown both sides.

LOBSTER WITH GOLD CHANTERELLES

3 live lobsters (1 ¼ pounds
  each)
½ pound gold or regular
  chanterelles, cleaned*
1 cup white wine vinegar
1 cup dry white wine
¾ cup sauterne or other wine
5 shallots, diced
½ cup whipping cream
½ pound unsalted butter
Salt and freshly ground black
  pepper to taste
¼ cup snipped fresh chives

In a large pot filled with boiling
salted water steam lobsters
about 10 minutes. Refresh the
lobsters in ice water and when
cool remove the meat from the
shell. With a mallet, crack the
cooked lobster shells to use in
the sauce.

Slice chanterelles lengthwise
into thin slices. In a separate
pan, place the vinegar, white
wine, ½ cup of the sauterne
and half of the shallots. Add
cracked lobster shells and boil
until the liquid is reduced to ¼
cup. Strain, discarding shells.
Return sauce to pan, add
cream and reduce until it thickens. Whisk in all but 2 tablespoons of the butter, a tablespoon at a time. Season with
salt and pepper.

In a large skillet sauté the
chanterelles in 2 tablespoons
butter with remaining shallots
for 3 to 4 minutes. Add the lobster meat (tails cut in half) and
deglaze with remaining ¼ cup
sauterne. Arrange on individual plates, nap with sauce and
sprinkle with chives. Makes 4
servings.

*Available at specialty produce or
gourmet markets.

BERRY PLATE WITH DOUBLE CREAM

Cluster in small mounds on
dessert plates five or six kinds
of berries: raspberries,
strawberries, red currants,
gooseberries, blueberries and
huckleberries. Spoon a dollop
of double cream or Crème
Fraîche (page 146) alongside.
Accompany with shortbread
cookies or almond wafers.

Anne Powning Haskel
Patricia Unterman
HAYES STREET GRILL
San Francisco, California

San Francisco's always-bustling Hayes Street Grill has built its fame on superb grilled fish specialties. Also extremely popular with grill patrons are its choice meats and charcuterie, like homemade whiskey and fennel sausages and boudin blanc, its salad table and the pastry cart.

Pots of palms and orchids lend a regal note to the busy ambience in this high-ceilinged, wood-floored bistro. A long bar, offering a notable selection of fine wines by the glass, cushions a wait for a table.

The talented kitchen staff is directed by two bright young

Anne Powning Haskel

women: Anne Powning Haskel, 33, and Patricia Unterman, 36. Together they blend their knowledge of international cuisine to set forth fresh, fast, down-to-earth fare.

Haskel favors the cooking of France, Italy and other European countries. Unterman's forte is the Orient, zeroing in on a Balinese dish or an Indonesian sate. Also regularly available are a wealth of dishes with a California stamp: warm Sonoma goat cheese salad, California pinot noir cioppino, leeks vinaigrette with local feta, fresh fruit ices in such flavors as kiwi, papaya, mint, pear or apple.

The pair alternate chef duties. Along with two other owners, Robert Flaherty and Richard Sander, they oversee a staff of fifty-five.

A graduate of the University of California, Berkeley, Haskel worked briefly as a paralegal aide before taking off to travel in Europe and South America. She apprenticed at the Charcuterie Cordier in Paris and Baque in Tarbes, France and had additional on-the-job training in several Bay Area restaurants.

Unterman graduated from Stanford in 1969 and then earned a master's degree in journalism from the University of California, Berkeley, in 1972. She studied cooking with Josephine Araldo in San Francisco and was part-owner and cook at Beggar's Banquet in Berkeley for six years. Unterman and Haskel worked together there before opening Hayes Street Grill in 1979. An offspring, Vicolo Pizzeria, opened in January 1984, specializing in deep-dish pizzas served in a fast food counter style.

AN AUTUMN DINNER

Warm Mushroom Salad

Grilled Marinated Rabbit

Pear Tart

WARM MUSHROOM SALAD

1 ½ pounds mixed shiitake, chanterelles and domestic mushrooms, sliced ⅛ -inch thick
3 tablespoons olive oil
1 ½ tablespoons sherry wine vinegar
Salt and freshly ground black pepper to taste
Butter lettuce leaves

In a large skillet over medium-high heat sauté mushrooms in oil until just cooked, about 4 minutes. Add wine vinegar and salt and pepper; heat, stirring, 1 minute. Arrange butter lettuce on individual plates and spoon over the hot mushrooms. Makes 4 servings.

GRILLED MARINATED RABBIT

1 rabbit (3 pounds) cut in
  serving pieces (or a 3-pound
  broiler-fryer, cut up)
1 can (3 ounces) green
  peppercorns
½ cup olive oil
3 garlic cloves, chopped
1 tablespoon lemon juice
3 tablespoons Dijon-style
  mustard
½ cup whipping cream

Wash rabbit and pat dry. Mash green peppercorns in a large bowl and stir in oil, garlic and lemon juice. Add rabbit pieces and let marinate in the refrigerator at least 12 hours, turning occasionally.

Grill over hot mesquite coals until cooked through, about 15 to 20 minutes. Do not overcook. Combine mustard and cream in a small saucepan, heat and serve with the grilled rabbit. Makes 4 servings.

PEAR TART

9-inch sugar crust Tart Shell,
  pre-baked ¾ (page 150)
Pears Poached in Red Wine
  (following)
¼ pound butter, softened
½ cup sugar
2 eggs
1 cup ground blanched
  almonds
¼ cup all-purpose flour

Prepare sugar crust tart shell. Poach pears. For filling, in a small bowl cream butter and sugar until light and fluffy. Beat in eggs, one at a time. Add nuts and flour, mixing well. Spread over tart shell. Slice pears ¼ -inch thick and arrange in concentric circles on top. Bake in a 350°F. oven for 30 minutes or until set and lightly browned. Serve at room temperature. Makes 8 servings.

PEARS POACHED IN RED WINE
Peel and core 2 Bartlett or Bosc pears. Place in a saucepan with 1 cup dry red wine and ¼ cup sugar. Bring to a boil and simmer for 15 minutes, turning pears occasionally, until pears are just cooked. Let cool.

A SUMMER DINNER

Cantaloupe, Figs and
Sonoma Cottage Ham

Oriental Swordfish and
Vegetable Brochettes

Asti Spumante Ice

CANTALOUPE, FIGS AND SONOMA COTTAGE HAM

1 ripe sweet cantaloupe
8 black Mission or green
  Adriatic figs
8 very thin slices high quality
  lightly smoked ham

Peel, halve and seed melon,
then slice. Halve figs. On four
plates arrange attractively the
melon slices, fig halves and
overlapping slices of ham.
Makes 4 servings.

ORIENTAL SWORDFISH AND VEGETABLE BROCHETTES

Ginger-Soy Marinade
(following)
1 ½ pounds fresh swordfish,
  cut in 1-ounce pieces
8 slices zucchini (each 1-inch
  thick), blanched
8 pieces red onion, blanched
8 squares sweet red pepper,
  blanched
8 mushrooms, cleaned and
  stems trimmed
8 cherry tomatoes

Prepare Ginger-Soy Marinade.
Place marinade in a bowl, add
swordfish pieces, and marinate
in the refrigerator for 6 hours,
turning occasionally. Alternate
pieces of fish and vegetables on
skewers, allowing 2 skewers
per person. Broil or grill over
hot mesquite coals for about 5
minutes, or until just cooked
through, turning frequently.
Makes 4 servings.

GINGER-SOY MARINADE Stir together 4 chopped garlic cloves,
1 tablespoon chopped fresh
ginger root, 1 teaspoon dry
mustard, ¼ cup chili-sesame
oil,* ½ cup soy sauce, juice of 2
lemons, 2 tablespoons rice
wine vinegar,* ¾ cup peanut
oil and cayenne to taste.

Available at Oriental markets.

ASTI SPUMANTE ICE

¾ cup sugar
1 cup water
2 cups good quality asti
  spumante
1 tablespoon fresh lemon juice
1 egg white

Combine sugar and water in a
saucepan, bring to a boil and
simmer until sugar is dissolved; let cool. Stir in asti spumante and lemon juice. Churn
in an ice cream freezer following manufacturer's instructions
for 15 minutes. Whip egg white
until frothy, fold into ice and
continue freezing 10 minutes
longer or until frozen. Makes
about 1 quart.

Patricia A. Wallesverd
JAMIESON HOUSE
Poynette, Wisconsin

The dining room of the elegant Victorian-style Jamieson House in Poynette, Wisconsin, features international cuisine with a five-course menu that changes weekly.

Owners Jeffrey Smith and Patricia A. Wallesverd present a luxurious style for their guests both at the table and in the guest house. White linen placemats, rose-patterned china, silver flatware and crys-

tal glasses set a sparkling table. Upon arrival guests are seated and served kir, a house aperitif. A choice of hors d'oeuvres, soup, entrée and a light salad follow. Entrées feature prime beef filet, pork and veal tenderloins, sweetbreads and fresh seafood.

Dessert and after-dinner liqueurs are served in the more informal garden room. Furnished with white wrought iron chairs, glass-topped tables and lush green plants, this bright and airy room also features a Tiffany stained-glass liqueur bar from a Mississippi riverboat.

The house chef is Wallesverd, a former model. Her cooking career is an extension of her background in fine arts with a degree from the University of Wisconsin in ceramics. Her culinary style reflects three trips around the world. She is famous for her desserts, and a line of them are sold to fine restaurants and specialty shops in Milwaukee and Chicago. Notable are chocolate fantasy, raspberry satin, almond mocha torte, white chocolate kiwi cake, amaretto bombe, banana tarts and kirsch genoise torte.

AN AUTUMN DINNER

Stuffed Grape Leaves

French Onion Soup

Pork Tenderloins with Cherry Wine Sauce

Pilaf

Herbed Green Beans

Apricot Hazelnut Torte

STUFFED GRAPE LEAVES

1 jar (8 ounces) preserved
  grape leaves, drained*
¾ pound ground lamb
2 tablespoons raw rice
1 garlic clove, minced
¼ teaspoon freshly ground
  black pepper
½ teaspoon ground cinnamon
½ teaspoon ground allspice
1 tablespoon chopped fresh
  mint
2 tablespoons water
2 cups Chicken Stock (page
  147)
3 tablespoons fresh lemon juice
Plain yogurt

Bring water to a boil in a large
pot. Drop in grape leaves, immediately remove and drain
well. Remove stems from
leaves. Pat dry with paper tow-
els. In a mixing bowl combine
lamb, rice, garlic, pepper, cinnamon, allspice and mint.
Sprinkle with water and mix
lightly. Place a rounded teaspoon of filling in the center of
each leaf, shiny surface down.
Fold like an envelope. Roll up
loosely and place in a saucepan. Pour in stock and add
lemon juice. Weight down with
a baking dish. Cover and sim-

mer 45 minutes. Let cool and
chill. Serve cold, several on
each plate, accompanied by a
spoonful of yogurt. Makes 8
servings.

*Available at gourmet markets and
Middle Eastern delicatessens.*

FRENCH ONION SOUP

4 large onions, thinly sliced
4 tablespoons unsalted butter
⅓ cup brandy
1 ½ quarts Beef Broth (page
  147)
1 ½ cups dry red wine
Freshly ground black pepper to
  taste
Slices of dry French bread
Grated Gruyère cheese

In a large soup pot sauté onions in butter until translucent.
Reduce heat, cover pan and let
onions cook slowly. When onions have released most of their
juices, uncover pan, turn up
heat and begin to caramelize
onions. Stirring occasionally,
cook about 30 minutes or until
onions have a golden, caramelized color. Stir in brandy. Add
broth and wine. Cover and

simmer 30 minutes. Season
with pepper. Ladle into bowls,
top with a slice of French
bread, sprinkle with cheese
and place under the broiler
briefly to melt the cheese.
Makes 6 to 8 servings.

NOTE The flavors of the soup
are enhanced when made a
day or two in advance.

PORK TENDERLOINS
WITH CHERRY WINE
SAUCE

6 pork tenderloins (about 2
  pounds)
2 tablespoons ground
  coriander
1 tablespoon ground
  cardamom
2 tablespoons soy sauce
1 tablespoon butter or
  vegetable oil
2 tablespoons Dijon-style
  mustard
Fine dry bread crumbs
Cherry Wine Sauce (following)

Trim any extra fat from the
meat and sprinkle with coriander, cardamom and soy. In a
large skillet brown tenderloins
in butter over medium-high
heat, turning to brown both

sides. Remove from heat, spread each tenderloin with about 1 teaspoon mustard and sprinkle lightly with bread crumbs. Transfer to a baking dish. Bake in a 350°F. oven for 15 to 20 minutes or until juicy and still slightly pink. Spoon Cherry Wine Sauce onto a platter and place tenderloins on the sauce. Makes 6 servings.

CHERRY WINE SAUCE In a saucepan sauté ½ cup chopped onion in ¼ teaspoon sesame oil until glazed. Add ½ cup rosé wine, ¼ cup port, ½ cup Chicken Stock (page 147), 1 cup drained pitted sour cherries, ¼ teaspoon cardamom, 2 minced small garlic cloves and a 1-inch piece of pickled hot and sour ginger or 1 tablespoon minced ginger root. Simmer until liquid is reduced by half. Puree in a food processor or blender until smooth. Add 1 cup whipping cream, return to a saucepan and simmer until sauce is reduced to a medium thickness.

APRICOT HAZELNUT TORTE

1 ½ cups apricot jam
6 dried apricot halves or 3 fresh apricots, pitted
¼ pound butter
1 cup sugar
7 eggs, separated
⅓ cup light rum
1 ¾ cups finely ground hazelnuts
½ cup fine dry bread crumbs
Whipped cream for garnish

In a blender or food processor puree jam and dried or fresh apricots. Set aside. Cream butter with ½ cup sugar until light and fluffy. Add egg yolks, beating well. Add rum. Beat egg whites until soft peaks form and gradually beat in remaining ½ cup sugar. Continue beating until whites are stiff and shiny but not dry. Mix together the hazelnuts and bread crumbs and fold into the egg yolk batter. Fold egg whites into the batter, one-third at a time.

Butter and flour the bottom only of a 9-inch springform pan. Pour half the batter into the prepared pan and bake in a 350°F. oven for 15 minutes, or

until cake is set enough to support the apricot puree. Gently spoon half of the apricot puree evenly over the cake to within ½ -inch of the sides of the pan. Spoon remaining cake batter over puree, taking care not to stir puree and batter together. Return cake to a 350°F. oven and continue baking 30 to 35 minutes longer, or until the cake turns golden and the center tests clean when a toothpick is inserted. Remove cake from oven and immediately run a thin-bladed knife around the sides of the pan. Let cake cool in pan on a wire rack.

When cake is cool, remove sides of springform pan. Heat remaining apricot puree until warm. Spoon over top of cake. Garnish with whipped cream rosettes and serve with additional whipped cream, if desired. Makes 16 servings.

A SPRING DINNER

Boerek

Filet Mignons with Green Peppercorns

Chocolate Strawberry Tarts

BOEREK*

½ pound feta cheese
¼ pound cream cheese
⅛ teaspoon nutmeg
2 eggs
Filo dough (about 6 sheets)
Melted unsalted butter

Using a food processor or mixer, cream cheeses together. Add nutmeg then eggs, one at a time, beating until smooth. Lay out 1 sheet of filo (keep the remainder covered with plastic wrap or a damp towel). Brush lightly with melted butter and cut into 6 strips, each about 3 inches wide. Drop a rounded teaspoon of filling on the lower corner of each strip of dough. Fold over to form a triangle and continue folding until end of strip. Lay on a buttered baking sheet. Repeat with remaining filo and brush tops of triangles with butter. Bake in a 350°F. oven for 15 to 20 minutes or until golden brown. Serve hot or reheat. Makes about 3 dozen. Serve 3 to 4 per person.

*Boerek is a Turkish word for a savory pastry or dumpling made with super-thin dough and filled with cheese, meat or chicken.

FILET MIGNONS WITH GREEN PEPPERCORNS

2 filet mignons, about 6 ounces each
1 to 2 tablespoons butter
½ cup dry red wine or port
¾ cup whipping cream
20 green peppercorns

Using a heavy skillet or saucepan, sear filets in butter over high heat, turning to brown both sides and cooking about 3 to 4 minutes or until medium rare. Remove to a platter and keep warm. Pour the wine into the pan and reduce by half. Add the cream and continue to reduce by half. Add the peppercorns and return the filets to the pan to warm in the sauce. Place the filets on plates and pour over the sauce. Makes 2 servings.

CHOCOLATE STRAWBERRY TARTS

6 ounces sweet chocolate
6 tablespoons unsalted butter
2 eggs, separated

¼ cup Grand Marnier or other orange-flavored liqueur
6 partially-baked Tart Shells (page 150)
Chocolate-dipped Strawberries for garnish (following)
Whipped cream for garnish

In a double boiler melt the chocolate and butter over hot water; remove from heat. Stir in the egg yolks and liqueur. Beat egg whites until stiff, but not dry, and fold in. Spoon into tart shells. Bake in a 350°F. oven for 20 to 25 minutes or until set through. Let cool and refrigerate. At serving time garnish with Chocolate-dipped Strawberries, injected with Grand Marnier, if desired, and decorate with whipped cream. Makes 6 to 8 servings.

CHOCOLATE-DIPPED STRAWBERRIES In a double boiler place 4 ounces chopped semisweet chocolate and 2 tablespoons orange-flavored liqueur and heat over hot water, stirring to blend. Dip a dozen large strawberries halfway into the chocolate. Place dipped fruit on a foil-lined pan, placing berries stem end down. Chill until chocolate sets.

John Ash
JOHN ASH & CO.
RESTAURANT AND
WINE SHOP
Santa Rosa, California

"A refugee from the corporate world, that's my background," quips John Ash, 41, owner-chef of a combination restaurant and wine shop in Santa Rosa, California, that bears his name.

Before opening his restaurant in September, 1980, Ash worked for Del Monte Corporation in San Francisco. His field was new product development and marketing. "Perhaps I had corporate burnout," says Ash, "but I wanted to do something more immediate in gratification and satisfaction. I had always loved to cook and was always involved with it." That became his direction.

After leaving Del Monte, Ash traveled to Europe and studied cooking at La Varenne in Paris and at Cordon Bleu in London. He then worked with a number of restaurant chefs throughout France. After two-and-a-half years, he returned to California to start anew. A

fine arts major in college, Ash became a freelance medical illustrator and a San Francisco caterer. He launched two small restaurants before his present venture.

Located in a flower-bedecked shopping complex with redwood exterior, John Ash & Co. ties in serenely with its surroundings. The restaurant's high-ceilinged white-washed interior exudes a light, airy, French country feeling. Turn-of-the-century French advertising posters adorn the walls. On the tables, white cloths and napkins and large white plates are set off by white-dotted navy blue undercloths.

Guests may browse in the wine shop while waiting for a table or sip a new release chosen from among the approximately fifteen wines available daily by the glass. "Wine should be affordable and pleasurable," Ash believes and so he features premium wines by the glass at the table and adds only a modest markup to wines by the bottle.

"Our emphasis is on the freshest things possible from

all over the world," claims Ash. That means fresh fish from Norway and Finland and choice produce from Australia and Chile. Local wild mushrooms—shiitake, chanterelles and morels—plus lots of game birds such as quail, pheasant and chukker, augment the stylish menu.

First courses encompass smoked Coho salmon with roasted walnut oil and capers; escargot with Roquefort butter; and assorted pâtés and terrines. Linguine with fresh mussels, breast of chicken with a ginger-tamari glaze and lamb chops with Taleggio are entrée specialties.

Although his medium is now cuisine, Ash sees a strong connection between his education as a painter and his vocation as a chef. "Art is very important to me, and pushing food around on a plate is like painting—it takes care of that need to do things that are pretty," says Ash.

AN AUTUMN MENU

Spinach and Shiitake Salad

Goat Cheese Fettuccine with Smoked Salmon

Baked Apples Marzipan

SPINACH AND SHIITAKE SALAD

½ pound shiitake or domestic mushrooms, sliced or diced
3 tablespoons olive oil
2 tablespoons lemon juice
Salt and freshly ground black pepper to taste
1 bunch spinach
½ cup plain yogurt
1 ½ tablespoons fresh lemon juice
1 teaspoon fresh lemon thyme or ¼ teaspoon dried dill

In a bowl toss shiitake mushrooms with oil, 2 teaspoons of the lemon juice and salt and pepper to taste. Let stand 10 minutes. Spread out spinach leaves on individual plates. Spoon over the mushrooms. Stir together the yogurt, remaining 4 teaspoons lemon juice and thyme. Spoon dressing over the salad. Makes 4 servings.

GOAT CHEESE
FETTUCCINE
WITH SMOKED SALMON

3 egg yolks
3 ounces goat cheese
⅔ cup whipping cream
¼ teaspoon freshly grated nutmeg
¼ teaspoon freshly ground black pepper
10 ounces fettuccine
8 ounces smoked salmon

In a saucepan beat together egg yolks, cheese, cream, nutmeg and pepper. Heat over very low heat until warm. Cook fettuccine in a large pot of boiling salted water until just tender. Drain and toss with warm goat cheese mixture. Garnish with smoked salmon slices. Makes 3 to 4 servings.

BAKED APPLES MARZIPAN

4 large baking apples
1 cup ground blanched almonds
¼ cup firmly packed brown sugar
1 egg
2 teaspoons dark rum
1 ½ tablespoons butter, melted
Crème Anglaise (page 146)

Core apples and peel one-third of the way down. Mix together almonds, sugar, egg and rum. With the nut mixture fill the apples and coat the peeled area on the outside of the apples. Place apples in a baking pan. Drizzle with melted butter. Bake in a 425°F. oven for 30 to 35 minutes or just until apples are tender. Serve warm or at room temperature with crème anglaise. Makes 4 servings.

A LATE SUMMER DINNER

Toasted Walnut
and Romaine Hearts Salad

Crab in Marsala

French Bread

Figs with Ricotta and
Chocolate Shavings

TOASTED WALNUT AND ROMAINE HEARTS SALAD

¼ cup coarsely chopped
   walnuts
½ cup walnut oil
1 small garlic clove, slightly
   crushed
1 ½ teaspoons red wine
   vinegar
¼ teaspoon salt
Pinch white pepper
4 Romaine hearts

In a small baking dish toast the walnuts in a 300°F. oven for 10 minutes or until lightly browned. Combine nuts, walnut oil and garlic and let sit at room temperature 24 hours. Just before serving stir in the vinegar, salt and pepper. Lay out Romaine hearts on individual salad plates. Spoon dressing and nuts over the greens, adding just enough dressing to coat lightly. Makes 4 servings.

CRAB IN MARSALA

½ cup dry marsala or vermouth
1 ⅓ cups Chicken Stock (page
   147)
1 tablespoon each chopped
   garlic and minced parsley
1 ½ teaspoons each soy sauce
   and fresh lemon juice
1 teaspoon sugar
2 tablespoons butter
2 teaspoons cornstarch
   dissolved in 2 teaspoons cold
   water
1 cleaned, cracked crab (about
   2 ½ pounds)
French bread for
   accompaniment

In a large saucepan combine the marsala, chicken stock, garlic, parsley, soy, lemon juice, sugar and butter. Bring to a boil and stir in the cornstarch paste. Cook, stirring, until thickened. Cover and simmer 10 minutes. Just before serving, add crab and heat through. Serve in deep bowls accompanied by French bread. Makes 2 servings.

FIGS WITH RICOTTA AND CHOCOLATE SHAVINGS

1 cup ricotta cheese
½ teaspoon grated lemon peel
⅛ teaspoon salt
¾ teaspoon vanilla extract
¼ cup sugar
1 egg white
12 large ripe figs
6 whole blanched almonds for
   garnish
Bittersweet chocolate shavings
   for garnish

Beat together the cheese, lemon peel, salt, vanilla and sugar. Beat egg white until soft peaks form and fold in. Slice figs into tulips and arrange 2 figs per serving on individual dessert plates. Pipe the ricotta mixture into the center of each fig. Top with almonds and chocolate shavings. Makes 6 servings.

John Clancy
JOHN CLANCY'S RESTAURANT
New York City, New York

New York restaurateur John Clancy, 53, is celebrating thirty years in the food realm. First a cooking teacher, he later founded his own New York school, John Clancy's Kitchen Workshop, and then started writing cookbooks. His fifth book is now underway.

In 1981, he opened John Clancy's Restaurant, designed with a blend of high tech and art deco, mirrors, white brick, prints, gray walls, white bentwood chairs, and tables draped with white cloths and pink underliners.

The restaurant was the first on the East Coast to cook with mesquite wood. Clancy credits the inspiration to a visit to a California home where friends grilled the dinner in this fashion.

The restaurant is open for dinner seven nights a week, offering seafood only. They cure their own gravlax and are noted for soups, in particular the lobster bisque. Other specialties include fisherman's stew with five kinds of shellfish, barbecued skewered jumbo shrimp, swordfish broiled over mesquite, lobster à l'Americaine, and Portuguese clams with linguica and serrano ham.

Desserts receive rave reviews, especially the English sherry trifle; individual lemon tarts; and the chocolate velvet cake, a composite of genoise soaked in Grand Marnier, triple-strength chocolate mousse and a cap of whipped cream.

A SUMMER DINNER

Bay Scallop Seviche

Grilled Skewered Swordfish with Bay Leaves

Potatoes Anna

Broccoli Mold

Chocolate Roulade

BAY SCALLOP SEVICHE

1 cup fresh lime juice
1 cup fresh lemon juice
¼ teaspoon dried red pepper flakes
1 red onion, sliced very thin
1 garlic clove, minced
¼ cup chopped fresh cilantro
1 ½ pounds bay scallops
Butter lettuce
Sliced tomato
Cilantro sprigs for garnish

Mix together in a bowl the lime juice, lemon juice, pepper flakes, onion, garlic and cilantro. Add scallops and let marinate in the refrigerator for 2 hours or not longer than 6 hours. Spoon onto butter lettuce and garnish with tomato slices and cilantro sprigs. Makes 6 servings.

GRILLED SKEWERED SWORDFISH WITH BAY LEAVES

1 large onion, grated
¼ cup lemon juice
1 teaspoon salt
½ teaspoon freshly ground
  black pepper
¼ cup olive oil
2 to 2 ½ pounds swordfish, cut
  in 1 ½ -inch cubes
24 bay leaves

In a large bowl stir together the onion, lemon juice, salt, pepper and oil. Add fish cubes and let marinate at least 2 hours. Meanwhile in a saucepan cover bay leaves with water, bring to a boil and remove from heat. Let cool to room temperature; drain. Arrange swordfish and bay leaves alternately on skewers. Grill over hot coals or broil for 6 to 8 minutes or just until fish is barely cooked through. Makes 6 servings.

CHOCOLATE ROULADE

8 ounces semisweet chocolate,
  coarsely chopped
¼ cup strong coffee
6 eggs, separated
¾ cup sugar
1 teaspoon vanilla extract
Whipped Cream Filling
  (following)
Chocolate Glaze (following),
  optional
½ cup toasted sliced almonds

Place chocolate and coffee in a double boiler and heat over hot water, stirring, until blended. Remove from heat and let cool to room temperature. In a large bowl beat egg whites until they hold soft peaks. Gradually add sugar and beat until stiff. Beat egg yolks until thick and light in color, add vanilla, and stir into the cooled chocolate. Using a spatula, fold ⅓ of the whites into the chocolate mixture to lighten it. Pour remaining whites into chocolate mixture and fold together gently. Grease an 11-by-17-inch jelly roll pan, line with buttered wax paper and pour in the batter. Bake in a 350°F. oven for 16 to 18 minutes or until set and a toothpick inserted comes out clean. Place pan on a rack and cover with a tea towel; let cool 10 minutes. Place the towel on the counter, cover with a sheet of wax paper, and invert cake onto the wax paper; peel off paper. Let cool completely. Spread with Whipped Cream Filling and roll up jelly roll fashion from a lengthwise side. Place on a serving platter. If desired, frost with Chocolate Glaze and sprinkle with nuts. Refrigerate. Let stand at room temperature 30 minutes before serving. Makes 8 servings.

WHIPPED CREAM FILLING Whip 1 ½ cups whipping cream until soft peaks form; beat in 3 tablespoons confectioners' sugar and 2 tablespoons cognac or brandy and continue to beat until stiff.

CHOCOLATE GLAZE (optional) In a double boiler heat 6 ounces coarsely chopped semisweet chocolate, 3 tablespoons soft butter and 2 tablespoon honey over hot water, stirring, until blended.

Michael Watren
LA PALME
The Newporter
Newport Beach, California

La Palme in Newport Beach offers "a return to freshness, simplicity and originality in dining," claims chef Michael Watren, 29. His secret—to blend the classic French tradition of preparation and presentation with California style.

"California nouvelle cuisine is an eclectic combination of the world's finest cuisines," explains Watren. "What we have done is to personalize our cuisine with many different influences—pasta from Italy, spicy dishes from Mexico and classic cuisine from France. Nothing is disguised. It is very clean and open, with a natural presentation."

La Palme capitalizes on California's abundant native products for appetizers, soups, pastas, salads, plus grilled entrées. Desserts are very light, emphasizing fresh fruits, fruit tarts and various daily specialties.

On the menu might be fresh tuna sashimi with seed mustard mousseline, baked goat cheese with watercress vinaigrette, stone crab and artichoke soup, roasted squab with grapes and cucumbers, and shrimp and lotte on a skewer with red bell pepper cream.

The ambience is California, sophisticated yet casual. Palm trees harmonize with contemporary ceramic artwork depicting the palm motif. The setting, overlooking a tiled courtyard, creates a stylish, breezy atmosphere for lunch, dinner and Sunday brunch.

Watren graduated from the Culinary Institute of America and previously served as chef of Bernard's restaurant at the Los Angeles Biltmore hotel.

A SUMMER MENU

Salad of Smoked Quail, Radicchio and Asparagus

Fettuccine with Leek, Pancetta and Tomato

Timbale of Goat Cheese with Fresh Fruit

SALAD OF SMOKED QUAIL, RADICCHIO AND ASPARAGUS

Raspberry Vinaigrette (following)
1 pound medium asparagus, trimmed and cooked crisply tender and chilled
1 medium head radicchio*
4 heads limestone lettuce
2 bunches watercress
6 bunches lambs lettuce
6 smoked quail, meat removed from bones and julienned or 1 ½ cups roasted duck or chicken, julienned
1 cup fresh raspberries
6 carrot flowers (made by cutting carrot slices with a tiny scalloped cutter)
3 tablespoons toasted sesame seeds

Prepare Raspberry Vinaigrette. Marinate asparagus in enough Raspberry Vinaigrette to coat. Wash greens well and break or separate into bite-sized pieces. Toss together with enough Raspberry Vinaigrette to coat lightly. Place greens on salad plates and top with smoked quail. Garnish with marinated asparagus, raspberries, and carrot flowers. Sprinkle with toasted sesame seeds. Makes 6 servings.

RASPBERRY VINAIGRETTE In a bowl whisk together ¼ cup raspberry vinegar, ¾ cup extra virgin olive oil, 1 teaspoon Dijon-style mustard and salt and freshly ground black pepper to taste.

A reddish-colored green usually imported from Italy.

FETTUCCINE WITH LEEK, PANCETTA AND TOMATO

1 pound pancetta, diced*
2 tablespoons extra virgin olive oil
2 medium leeks, trimmed and diced
1 medium tomato, peeled, seeded and chopped
1 ½ teaspoons minced garlic
1 ½ pounds fresh fettuccine
Salt and freshly ground black pepper to taste
2 tablespoons minced fresh chives or green onion tops

In a large skillet sauté pancetta in olive oil until crisp. Remove pancetta from pan, add leeks and tomato and cook until soft. Add garlic and cook 1 minute. Meanwhile, cook pasta in boiling salted water until just tender; drain. In a large bowl mix together the pasta with the pancetta and tomato-leek mixture. Season with salt and pepper. Spoon onto plates and top with minced chives. Makes 6 servings.

An Italian bacon available at Italian and gourmet markets.

TIMBALE OF GOAT CHEESE
WITH FRESH FRUIT

8 ounces California goat cheese
  (chèvre)
½ cup ricotta cheese
¼ cup whipping cream
2 tablespoons sugar
3 cups fresh fruit: raspberries,
  strawberries, sliced peaches
  or sliced kiwi, preferably a
  combination

In a food processor puree the
goat cheese, ricotta, cream and
sugar until smooth. Butter and
sugar 6 timbale molds (about 5-
ounce size) and spoon in the
cheese mixture. Tap to remove
any air. Cover with plastic
wrap and refrigerate at least 24
hours to firm up.

   To serve, dip the molds in
hot water for 5 seconds to
loosen and unmold on individual plates. Circle with fresh
fruit. Makes 6 servings.

A LATE SPRING MENU

Jícama Pancake with Smoked
Salmon and Caviar

Veal with Green Olives and
Shiitake Mushrooms

Grapefruit Mousse with
Strawberry Sauce

JICAMA PANCAKE
WITH SMOKED SALMON
AND CAVIAR

1 pound jícama, peeled and
  shredded or julienned
½ pound potatoes, peeled and
  shredded or julienned (1 large
  potato)
2 eggs, beaten
Salt and freshly ground black
  pepper to taste
2 tablespoons butter
6 ounces smoked salmon,
  julienned
½ cup sour cream
4 ounces caviar (optional)
Fresh dill sprigs

In a bowl mix together the jícama and potato. Squeeze out
any extra moisture, making the
mixture as dry as possible. Mix
in eggs and season with salt
and pepper. In a large skillet
melt butter and sauté mixture
over medium-high heat, tossing to cook through. Spoon
onto a platter. Garnish with
salmon strips and spoonfuls of
sour cream and caviar. Tuck dill
sprigs around the edge. Makes
4 servings.

VEAL WITH GREEN OLIVES AND SHIITAKE MUSHROOMS

4 veal tenderloins (4 to 6 ounces each)
Salt and freshly ground black pepper to taste
4 tablespoons butter
¾ pound shiitake mushrooms, stems removed and caps sliced
2 garlic cloves, minced
2 shallots, minced
1 ½ cups Veal Demi-Glace (page 148)
½ cup dry white wine
¼ cup sliced green olives
2 tablespoons minced fresh chives

Season veal with salt and pepper and sauté in 2 tablespoons of the butter in a large skillet, turning to brown both sides and cooking until medium rare. In another skillet sauté mushrooms in remaining butter with garlic and shallots. Add demi-glace, wine and olives and reduce until slightly thickened. Place veal on plates and spoon over sauce. Sprinkle with chives. Makes 4 servings.

GRAPEFRUIT MOUSSE WITH STRAWBERRY SAUCE

1 ½ teaspoons unflavored gelatin
2 tablespoons cold water
2 egg yolks
6 tablespoons sugar
6 tablespoons Crème Fraîche (page 146) or sour cream
½ cup frozen grapefruit juice concentrate, thawed
¾ cup whipping cream
4 mint sprigs for garnish
1 cup grapefruit sections for garnish
Strawberry Sauce (following)

Sprinkle gelatin into cold water and let stand until softened. Beat egg yolks and sugar until light in color, turn into a double boiler and stir in crème fraîche or sour cream and grapefruit juice concentrate. Cook over hot water, stirring, until custard coats spoon. Add softened gelatin and cool the mixture by setting pan in ice; stir. When cool, whip cream until stiff and fold in. Turn into four individual molds. Chill at least 12 hours.

To serve, dip molds in hot water for 5 seconds and unmold on plates. Spoon Strawberry Sauce around molds and garnish with mint sprigs and grapefruit. Makes 4 servings.

STRAWBERRY SAUCE In a food processor or blender puree 1 pint strawberries and press through a strainer. Stir in 2 tablespoons sugar and 2 tablespoons kirsch.

**Karl Schaefer
LE CUISINIER
Portland, Oregon**

Le Cuisinier in Portland, Oregon, excels in presenting indigenous seasonal products in highly imaginative dishes.

Chef/owner Karl Schaefer, 30, calls the Northwest "a culinary heaven."

Along with excellent greens and an incredible array of high quality fruits and vegetables, "there is every variety of berry you could ever want, fresh from the fields." Also readily obtained are fresh quail, Hungarian partridge, pheasant, rabbit, chickens, geese and prime local lamb and veal.

Excellent fish and shellfish are caught in the waters off the Oregon, Washington and Alaskan coasts. Schaefer utilizes the abundance of exotic fungi, great wild morels, fresh white truffles, cèpes and chanterelles, available to him. He points out the growing quality of locally-produced wines.

At Le Cuisinier, Schaefer intertwines this bounty in such appetizer specialties as smoked Oregon chinook salmon; shellfish ragout of oysters, clams, mussels, scallops and shrimp in a tarragon tomato broth; or quail pâté with fresh Oregon truffles. Popular entrées in the summertime are barbecued lamb tenderloin served with chilled ratatouille or paupiettes stuffed with smoked salmon mousse. Cassoulet, grilled fish with butter sauces and confit of duck are entrées highly favored by customers.

Fresh sorbets and ice creams, Grand Marnier soufflés, and chocolate tortes fill the dessert bill of fare.

One wall of the restaurant is mirror-lined; the others, painted off-white, serve as a gallery for Monet prints. On the tables, fresh flowers bedeck white cloths. The modest simplicity forms an understated backdrop for the stellar food.

Schaefer grew up in Wilmette, Illinois and began working in the kitchen at the Wilmette Country Club when he was fourteen years old. He was thrust into the lunch cook's job one day after another employee quit, and remained there for two summers, working the short order and prep cook stations at night.

During high school he held jobs in bakeries and restaurants until moving to New York and enrolling at the Culinary Institute of America. While in school he worked with a "wonderful, highly intelligent, skilled chef," Peter Van Erp, at the Dutchess Valley Rod and Gun Club in Pawling, New York. Then he apprenticed at Le Perroquet in New York with Pierre Poubelle, "an older, incredibly talented, classic French chef." Poubelle retired and was replaced by an American, Michael Beck, "a young, sublime artist as well as an excellent teacher." Schaefer cites these three men as being most responsible for his expertise today.

Schaefer left New York for Portland when his wife was accepted to graduate school there.

AN AUTUMN DINNER

Wild Mushrooms in Madeira and Brandy Cream Sauce

Roast Saddle of Lamb with Pureed Acorn Squash and Sugar Snap Peas

Late Harvest Raspberries with Crème Anglaise and Ladyfingers

WILD MUSHROOMS IN MADEIRA AND BRANDY CREAM SAUCE

1 ½ cups each of four types of mushrooms: chanterelles, cèpes, morels and domestic mushrooms*
1 ½ tablespoons butter
⅓ cup cognac or brandy
⅓ cup Madeira
1 cup whipping cream
2 tablespoons Glace de Viande (jellied meat glaze) (page 148)
1 teaspoon beurre manié (butter blended with 1 teaspoon flour)
4 Puff Pastry cases, 1 inch high (page 149)
Dash each cognac and Madeira
Chopped fresh parsley

Wipe mushrooms clean and slice ¼-inch thick, stems included. Using a large skillet sauté mushrooms in butter over high heat until they shed enough juice to just cover bottom of pan. Pour off juice and mushrooms and reserve. Add brandy and Madeira to the skillet and reduce by half. Lower heat to moderately high, add cream and glace de viande plus the reserved mushroom juice and reduce slightly. Add beurre manié, reduce heat and simmer gently 3 to 5 minutes, or until thickened. Place puff pastry on a baking sheet in a 350°F. oven and heat through, about 10 minutes. Add a dash of cognac and Madeira to the sauce and return mushrooms to the pan. Reheat and spoon inside puff pastry shells and sprinkle with parsley. Makes 4 servings.

Wild mushrooms are available at specialty produce markets.

ROAST SADDLE OF LAMB WITH PUREED ACORN SQUASH AND SUGAR SNAP PEAS

3 pound boned butterflied
  lamb loin or leg of lamb
Pine Nut and Olive Stuffing
  (following)
Pureed Acorn Squash
  (following)
Sugar snap peas for
  accompaniment

Prepare Pine Nut and Olive Stuffing. Lay out meat on a board and spread with stuffing. Roll up meat and tie with string. Place on a rack in a roasting pan, insert a meat thermometer and roast in a 425°F. oven for 15 minutes. Reduce heat to 325°F. and roast until the meat thermometer registers 145°F. for medium

rare, about 1 hour longer. Meanwhile, prepare Pureed Acorn Squash.

To serve, slice meat and accompany with Pureed Acorn Squash and hot sugar snap peas. If desired, accompany with a sauce made with deglazed lamb drippings and white wine. Makes about 6 to 8 servings.

PINE NUT AND OLIVE STUFFING
In a bowl mix together ¼ cup chopped Mediterranean-style olives, 2 minced garlic cloves, 1 tablespoon chopped fresh basil, 1 teaspoon chopped fennel greens, ½ cup toasted pine nuts and salt and freshly ground black pepper to taste.

PUREED ACORN SQUASH Halve 2 large acorn squash, remove seeds and place cut side down in a baking pan. Add 1 inch of water. Bake in a 350°F. oven for 1 hour, or until tender when pierced with a fork. Scoop squash from the shell and puree in a food processor with 1 cup whipping cream, salt, freshly ground black pepper and nutmeg to taste.

LATE HARVEST RASPBERRIES WITH CREME ANGLAISE AND LADYFINGERS

Crème Anglaise (page 146)
Raspberry Puree (following)
Raspberries
Ladyfingers

On each dessert plate spoon a layer of crème anglaise to cover the bottom. Then on top within the pool of crème anglaise make a circle of Raspberry Puree leaving a 1-inch border. Center the puree with fresh raspberries, about ½ cup for each plate. Complete the plate by arranging 5 or 6 ladyfingers in a fan on one side of the plate.

RASPBERRY PUREE In a food processor or blender puree 1 ½ cups raspberries, push through a sieve and sweeten to taste. Stir in 1 tablespoon framboise, if desired.

A SUMMER DINNER

Chilled Barbecued Quail on Limestone Lettuce

Paupiettes of Petrale Sole with Mousseline of Dungeness Crab

Huckleberry Sorbet in a Honeydew Melon

CHILLED BARBECUED QUAIL ON LIMESTONE LETTUCE

Tamari Sauce (following)
4 quail
Salt and freshly ground black pepper to taste
¼ cup Crème Fraîche (page 146)
1 teaspoon freshly grated horseradish or to taste
Limestone lettuce leaves, about 2 dozen

Prepare Tamari Sauce. Split quail lengthwise, remove part of the backbone and season with salt and pepper. Let rest 4 to 5 minutes. Grill quail over hot coals, basting with Tamari Sauce and grilling until browned and cooked through but still juicy, about 5 to 6 minutes. Chill. Mix together crème fraîche and horseradish. Fan a salad plate with lettuce leaves and place ½ teaspoon of crème fraîche mixture on leaves where stems touch. Place quail skin side up, with legs facing out, on the center of the plate. Makes 4 servings.

TAMARI SAUCE In a small bowl stir together ½ cup Veal Demi-Glace (page 148), ¼ cup tamari* and ¼ cup dry white wine. Grind 3 juniper berries in a mortar with 1 small garlic clove and add. Blend in 1 egg yolk.

*Available at Oriental markets.

PAUPIETTES OF PETRALE SOLE WITH MOUSSELINE OF DUNGENESS CRAB*

Crab Mousseline (following)
8 to 10 fillets of sole (4 to 5 ounces each), skinned
White wine
1 shallot, chopped
8 to 10 leaves fresh tarragon
Hollandaise or Beurre Blanc (page 146)
Garnish: asparagus tips, potatoes and crab claws (reserved from mousseline)

Prepare Crab Mousseline. Pound individual skinned fillets gently. Spread crab mousseline evenly on fillets. Roll up starting with the smaller end of fillet; tie with string. Place paupiettes in a large skillet with ⅓-inch of white wine, shallots and 1 tarragon leaf on each piece. Bring to a simmer, cover and place in a 350°F. oven about 6 minutes (fish will be underdone). Remove from oven and snip strings. Arrange 2 paupiettes on each plate and garnish with asparagus tips, potatoes dressed with melted butter and crab claws; spoon over hollandaise or beurre blanc. Makes 4 servings.

CRAB MOUSSELINE Fill an 8-to-10-quart pot two-thirds full of water and bring to a rapid boil. Drop in 1 live Dungeness crab and leave 1 ½ to 2 minutes. Remove to ice water. With mallet, crack and remove meat from the claws. Open and remove meat from the body. Reserve claws for garnish; use meat in mousseline. In a food processor puree 5 ounces crab meat, 3 ounces scallops and 1 egg white. Place in a stainless steel bowl set in ice. Blend in ½ cup whipping cream. Add 1 teaspoon cognac and ½ teaspoon fresh lemon juice. Season with salt and freshly ground black pepper to taste.

Paupiettes are thin slices of fish or meat that are stuffed, rolled and braised and baked.

HUCKLEBERRY SORBET IN A HONEYDEW MELON

4 cups huckleberries
1 cup sugar
¾ cup water
3 tablespoons fresh lemon juice
1 honeydew melon

Puree berries in a food processor or blender and press through a fine strainer. Bring sugar and water to a boil and cook until clear. Cool. Combine berries with sugar syrup and lemon juice. Chill. Churn in an ice cream freezer following manufacturer's instructions until frozen. Cut melon into wedges and scoop out seeds. Serve a melon wedge with a scoop of sorbet. Makes 8 servings.

Jimmy Schmidt
LONDON CHOP HOUSE
Detroit, Michigan

With dark brown leather banquettes and an old-fashioned bar the length of the room, the forty-five-year-old London Chop House in Detroit, Michigan, has the elegant ambience of an English club. The extensive luncheon and dinner menu is reprinted twice daily with changing specials. At night there is dinner music and dancing.

In charge is a handsome and talented young executive chef, Jimmy Schmidt, 28. He has been with the restaurant seven years and got his start in the storeroom.

After graduating from high school at sixteen, Schmidt attended the University of Illinois for two years and majored in electrical engineering. At eighteen he took off for France and enrolled in food classes in Avignon where Madeleine Kamman was his major instructor. After studying with her for a year, he followed Kamman to her Boston school and stayed on to manage her new restaurant, Chez la Mère Madeleine, for a year-and-a-half, before moving to Detroit.

The London Chop House dinner menu of over one hundred dishes includes terrines of veal and duck, gravlax of Norwegian salmon with dill sauce, green fettuccine with mushrooms, iced gazpacho and New England firehouse clam chowder. Some entrée specialties are a heap of frog legs roadhouse style, Maine scallop and shrimp fettuccine, sautéed veal Oscar II with Maine back fin crab and fresh asparagus, and grilled calves' liver with avocado.

Desserts list Lundt chocolate chestnut cake, coffee ice cream cake with hot fudge sauce, housemade cheese cake with fresh strawberry sauce and frozen chocolate soufflé with Grand Marnier.

A SUMMER MENU

Spinach Fettuccine Primavera

Medallions of Salmon with Basil Beurre Blanc

Limestone Lettuce Salad

White Chocolate Mousse with Raspberries

SPINACH FETTUCCINE PRIMAVERA

12 ounces spinach or egg fettuccine
1 bunch asparagus, tips cut off, stems sliced thinly
8 ounces chanterelles or domestic mushrooms, cleaned and cut if large
¼ pound butter
6 ounces baby green beans, cleaned and blanched
1 each sweet red and yellow bell pepper, peeled and julienned
Salt and white pepper to taste
½ cup chopped fresh chives or green onion tops
¼ cup chopped fresh tarragon or 1 ½ teaspoons dried tarragon
4 ounces (1 cup) freshly grated Parmesan cheese (preferably Parmigiano-Reggiana)

Cook the fettuccine in a large amount of boiling salted water. When pasta is barely tender, about 3 minutes, add the asparagus tips to the boiling fettuccine. Working quickly, in a skillet over medium-high heat sauté the asparagus stems and chanterelles in butter. Add the green beans and peppers and sauté just until hot. Season with salt and pepper. When the pasta is just tender, drain and immediately add to the vegetables. Toss. Add the chives and tarragon, adjust seasonings and heat 1 minute to let the aromas of the herbs exude. Remove from heat and toss with cheese. Serve on a platter or individual plates and sprinkle with cheese. Makes 4 servings.

MEDALLIONS OF SALMON WITH BASIL BEURRE BLANC

Court Bouillon (following)
Salmon fillet (1 ½ pounds), skinned
2 cups dry white wine
1 cup white wine vinegar or basil vinegar
1 cup shallots, coarsely chopped
1 tablespoon white peppercorns
1 bunch basil sprigs, chopped
½ pound unsalted butter, cut in pieces
3 to 4 ounces salmon caviar
1 cup julienne of mixed basil (sweet, lemon and dark opal varieties)

Prepare Court Bouillon and let cook at least 2 hours before using. Cut salmon fillet across the grain into eight equal sections. On a chopping board, place two of the sections positioning them exactly opposite the other with the inner spine side touching. Wrap each section around each other and secure with two toothpicks. Reserve.

To prepare sauce, in an acid-resistant saucepan combine the white wine, vinegar, shallots, peppercorns and basil sprigs. Reduce over high heat to ½ cup liquid. Strain through a fine sieve and reserve.

Place the salmon medallions into simmering Court Bouillon. Reduce heat and check salmon after 4 minutes. When no longer translucent, quickly remove from pan; remove toothpicks.

Meanwhile return sauce to a boil. Whisk in the butter, one piece at a time. Adjust seasonings and reduce to a light sauce consistency. When desired texture is reached, remove and whisk for a few seconds to stabilize. Add the caviar, stirring it gently into the sauce. Spoon sauce onto a serving platter. Sprinkle the julienne of basil evenly across; place the salmon medallions on top. Makes 4 servings.

COURT BOUILLON In a large acid-resistant saucepan combine 1 cup white wine vinegar, 3 cups dry white wine, 1 coarsely chopped onion, 1 tablespoon white peppercorns, 1 bay leaf and 1 small bunch of thyme or 1 tablespoon dried thyme. Add enough water to cover the fish. Bring to a boil and let simmer for at least 2 hours before poaching fish.

WHITE CHOCOLATE
MOUSSE WITH
RASPBERRIES

2 egg yolks
⅔ cup half-and-half
9 ounces white chocolate,
   broken into small pieces
10 tablespoons unsalted butter,
   at room temperature
1 pint raspberries
Sugar to taste
1 tablespoon framboise
   (optional)
Mint sprigs for garnish

Beat egg yolks until light and stir in half-and-half. Place in a double boiler and cook over hot water, stirring, until mixture coats a spoon. Remove from heat immediately, add chocolate, and stir until the chocolate is melted completely. Whisk in the butter, one tablespoon at a time. Turn into a pan, cover and freeze until solid, several hours or overnight. In a food processor or blender, puree half the raspberries, sweeten to taste and strain through a fine sieve. Stir in framboise, if desired. Refrigerate. To serve, pour a small pool of puree onto a plate. With two spoons mold a "quenelle" or oval scoop of white chocolate and arrange on sauce, making two or three for each serving. Position whole raspberries around the plate. Garnish with mint. Makes 6 to 8 servings.

A SPRING MENU

Morels and Asparagus
in Puff Pastry

Roast Rib of Young Lamb
with Rosemary

Potatoes Dauphinoise

Frozen Hazelnut Soufflé

MORELS AND ASPARAGUS IN PUFF PASTRY

1 pound fresh morel
  mushrooms, stems removed
  or domestic mushrooms
1 pound asparagus
8 ounces Puff Pastry, cut into 6
  rectangular or diamond
  shapes (page 149)
2 shallots, chopped
12 tablespoons unsalted butter
Salt and white pepper to taste
1 cup champagne
2 cups whipping cream
1 bunch watercress for garnish

If morels are very large, cut in half lengthwise. Wash very well under running cold water and let drain. Peel asparagus. Cut in lengths to the size of the puff pastry shells. Blanch asparagus in boiling salted water until just crisply tender; drain, reserving blanching water. Cool asparagus under cold water to stop the cooking; reserve. Bake the puff pastry shells in a 425°F. oven for 15 minutes or until golden brown. Let cool on a rack and split horizontally.

To prepare sauce, sauté shallots in 2 tablespoons butter in a saucepan until partially translucent. Add champagne, reserving 2 teaspoons, and reduce by half over medium-high heat. Add cream and reduce by half. Strain through a fine sieve and reserve.

To assemble, reheat the puff pastry shells in a 250°F. oven until hot through. Return the sauce to a boil. Gradually whisk in approximately 8 tablespoons of butter, one tablespoon at a time. Season with salt and white pepper. Lightly sauté the morels over medium-high heat in 2 tablespoons butter. Drain and add the drained juices to the sauce. Return the asparagus to the blanching water to reheat. Drain well. Remove the pastry shells from the oven. Place pastry bottoms onto a serving plate. Arrange the asparagus and morels in them.

Whisk 2 teaspoons champagne into the sauce, which should be a light consistency, and whisk a few seconds. Pour sauce over and into the morels, asparagus and pastry shells. Replace the puff pastry tops. Garnish the plate with watercress and serve. Makes 6 servings.

ROAST RIB
OF YOUNG LAMB
WITH ROSEMARY

1 ¾ cups cabernet sauvignon or
other dry red wine
1 shallot, chopped
2 garlic cloves
1 tablespoon white or black
peppercorns
¼ cup chopped parsley sprigs
½ teaspoon juniper berries
½ teaspoon whole allspice
¼ cup chopped fresh rosemary
or 1 tablespoon dried
rosemary
½ cup whipping cream
1 small garlic clove, minced
1 teaspoon grated lemon peel
1 cup Veal Demi-Glace (page
148)
2 racks of lamb (about 2
pounds each), well-trimmed
2 tablespoons butter
1 small celery root, peeled, cut
into "olives" and blanched
until crisply tender
⅓ cup lightly toasted pine nuts
1 ½ pounds rocket,* spinach or
red Swiss chard, coarsely
chopped and steamed,
seasoned with butter and salt

First prepare the sauce. It may
be done well in advance and
reheated to accompany the
meat, which takes a brief cooking time. For the wine reduction sauce, in a medium saucepan place the wine, shallot,
garlic, peppercorns, parsley
sprigs, juniper berries and allspice. Bring to a simmer and
reduce by ¾ the original volume. Strain through a fine
sieve and reserve. Add 2 tablespoons of the rosemary to the
cream and reduce by half over
medium-high heat. Strain and
reserve. Mix the remaining
rosemary with the garlic and
lemon peel; reserve.

In a saucepan combine the
demi-glace with the wine reduction sauce. Bring to a fast
simmer and let reduce to 1 cup
of light sauce consistency. Add
the cream and reduce back to
light sauce consistency.
Reserve.

Place meat on a rack in a
roasting pan and roast in a
450°F. oven for 15 minutes. Remove from oven and trim away
any fat. Return to oven until
desired temperature is
reached, 140°F. for rare and
145°F. for medium rare (about 5
to 10 minutes longer). Remove
from oven and let rest 15
minutes.

After lamb has rested, return
to a 450°F. oven and reheat to
desired temperature. Return
sauce to a simmer, add the
rosemary garnish mixture and
whisk in the butter. Adjust seasonings. Add the celery root
and pine nuts and heat
through.

Quickly reheat rocket, spinach or chard. To serve, first
spoon sauce onto a serving
plate. Arrange meat on top and
spoon a touch of the sauce
over. Accompany with rocket
and the Potatoes Dauphinoise.
Makes 6 servings.

NOTE The restaurant has the
ribs removed from the backbone so the meat can later be
carved into long thin slices and
arranged overlapping on each
plate. For ease at home, have
the rib bones cracked so the
ribs may be easily cut apart for
serving two to three per
person.

*Available in season at specialty
produce markets.

POTATOES DAUPHINOISE

6 medium potatoes
1 ½ tablespoons butter
Salt and freshly ground black
  pepper to taste
3 tablespoons chopped fresh
  parsley
1 garlic clove, minced
⅔ cup freshly grated Parmesan
  (preferably Parmigiano-
  Reggiana)
2 cups whipping cream

Peel and slice potatoes thinly.
Arrange one slightly overlapping layer in a well-buttered
baking dish. Sprinkle with salt
and pepper. Mix parsley and
garlic; scatter part over, and
add another layer of potatoes.
Sprinkle with part of the
cheese. Continue building alternating layers. Pour cream
over the top and finish with
cheese. Bake in a 350°F. oven
for 1 hour or until potatoes are
tender and golden brown.
Makes 6 servings.

FROZEN HAZELNUT SOUFFLE

2 teaspoons unflavored gelatin
½ cup frangelico or amaretto
6 egg yolks
6 tablespoons sugar
¼ teaspoon vanilla extract
Pinch salt
3 egg whites
1 ¾ cups whipping cream
Hazelnut Praline (following)

Place a lightly buttered collar of
parchment paper or foil around
a 1-quart soufflé mold. Freeze.
Combine gelatin and ¼ cup of
the frangelico or amaretto in a
small bowl; set in a larger bowl
partially filled with warm
water, to dissolve gelatin.

In a mixing bowl combine
the egg yolks, sugar, vanilla
and salt and beat with an electric mixer until the ribbon
stage. Stir in the melted gelatin. Whip egg whites until soft
peaks form and fold in the egg
yolk base. Whip the cream until soft peaks form and beat in
the remaining frangelico or
amaretto just until lightly
thickened. Fold cream into the
base. Pour into the soufflé
mold and freeze at least 8
hours. To serve, remove the
soufflé from the freezer and
cover the surface with the
chopped Hazelnut Praline. Un-
wrap the collar. Makes 8
servings.

HAZELNUT PRALINE In a heavy
saucepan heat ½ cup sugar
over medium-high heat until it
melts and caramelizes. Add ½
cup chopped hazelnuts and
shake to coat. Turn out on buttered foil and let cool. Chop
coarsely.

Mark Rosenstein
THE MARKET PLACE
Asheville, North Carolina

After studying photography and graphics at Northwestern University and the Rhode Island School of Design, Mark Rosenstein, 31, took a summer job as a carpenter's helper in the Blue Ridge Mountains of North Carolina. Friends had bought a grist mill in a remote area and were transforming it into a thirty-seat restaurant.

Upon completion of the construction work, Rosenstein "was tricked to stay on and do the cooking," he says merrily. A crash course with Irena Chalmers, a noted food authority and cookbook publisher living in the area, provided him with a basic culinary background.

When customers would ask for a specialty not on the menu, Rosenstein would turn to Escoffier and try out the dish. "That's really how I expanded my talents," he explains.

Rosenstein stayed at the Frog and Owl, located five miles down a one-lane dirt road and open for four months only during the summer season, for five years. Off-season he worked at resorts in Florida and also used the time to study with Simone Beck, who arranged an apprenticeship with Roger Vergé at Moulin de Mougins on the French Riviera.

Five years ago Rosenstein opened The Market Place in a former natural foods cafeteria in downtown Asheville. The ambience is eclectic, featuring handcrafted tiles, chintz draperies, and bamboo wood in the dining room. A grill room is oak paneled with brick trim. Candles and white tablecloths add formality.

Menu specialties include vegetable terrine and conch chowder for openers. Turbot in champagne sauce, crab soufflé in a crêpe, and loin of veal with chanterelles in cream sauce are entrées. For dessert, patrons can try marjolaine, raspberry and champagne sorbets, burnt honey ice cream and fresh fruit plate with sabayon and puff pastry.

"I'm a wine lover and I think dining is a very civilized thing to do," says Rosenstein. "Sharing at the table and the celebration people should have together, is a basic tenet of mine. It is really why I got interested in being a chef."

A SUMMER DINNER

Pasta with Mussels
and Tomatoes

Breast of Chicken
Stuffed with Spinach
and Prosciutto

Butter Lettuce Salad

Berries with Sabayon
and Puff Pastry

PASTA WITH MUSSELS AND TOMATOES

6 tablespoons diced shallots
2 tablespoons minced fresh
  parsley
2 tablespoons fresh oregano or
  1 ½ teaspoons dried oregano
½ cup Fish Stock (page 147)
½ cup dry white vermouth
½ cup dry white wine
2 large tomatoes, peeled,
  seeded and diced
Salt and freshly ground black
  pepper to taste
2 dozen mussels, steamed and
  shucked
8 ounces fresh fettuccine
Freshly grated Romano cheese
Freshly ground black pepper to
  taste

In a heavy saucepan combine
the shallots, parsley, oregano
and fish stock. Bring to a boil
and reduce by one-half. Add
vermouth, wine and tomatoes
and reduce by one-third. Season with salt and pepper and
keep warm. Just before serving
add mussels. Cook fettuccine
in a large pot of boiling salted
water until just tender, about 3
minutes; drain. Add the mus-
sel-tomato sauce and toss
lightly. Turn out on a hot platter or individual plates. Sprinkle with cheese and freshly
ground pepper. Makes 4
servings.

VARIATION Omit oregano and
reduce the amount of ver-
mouth and wine by one-half.
Add 1 cup whipping cream
and 1 teaspoon saffron to the
reduction.

BREAST OF CHICKEN STUFFED WITH SPINACH AND PROSCIUTTO

4 chicken breast halves (about 1½ pounds), boned and skinned
12 ounces fresh spinach, stems removed, and blanched
3 ounces finely diced prosciutto
3 ounces grated Gruyère cheese
Salt, freshly ground black pepper and nutmeg to taste
1 tablespoon butter
Béarnaise Sauce (following)

Pound chicken breasts lightly to flatten evenly. Chop the blanched, drained spinach and mix in a bowl with prosciutto and cheese. Season with salt, pepper and nutmeg. Place a mound of the spinach filling on each laid out breast, roll up, and tie with string. In a large skillet brown stuffed chicken breasts in butter over medium-high heat, turning to brown all sides.

Transfer chicken to a casserole and bake in a 400°F. oven for 20 minutes. Remove from oven and snip string from chicken. Slice each breast into 5 slices. Spoon Béarnaise Sauce onto a warm platter or individual plates. Arrange breast slices on sauce. Makes 4 servings.

BÉARNAISE SAUCE In a saucepan combine 2 tablespoons fresh tarragon, 2 tablespoons fresh chervil (optional), 2 tablespoons minced parsley, 4 tablespoons diced shallots, 2 tablespoons vinegar and ½ cup dry red wine. Bring to a boil and reduce liquid to 3 tablespoons (do not strain). Rinse a blender container with hot water to heat through, add 3 egg yolks and the reduced wine-herb mixture and blend. Gradually pour in 6 ounces butter, melted, and blend until smooth. Makes about 1 cup sauce.

BERRIES WITH SABAYON AND PUFF PASTRY

1 pint each strawberries, raspberries and blackberries or blueberries
3 egg yolks
½ cup sugar
1 cup champagne or riesling
2 teaspoons grated orange peel
1 tablespoon Grand Marnier
4 freshly baked Puff Pastry crescents or diamonds (page 149)

Clean and stem berries and arrange in individual serving dishes. For Sabayon, beat egg yolks in a double boiler and beat in sugar. Place over hot water and beat until yolks are thick. Heat champagne until steaming and blend into the yolk mixture. Continue cooking, whisking constantly, until mixture quadruples in volume. Add the orange peel and Grand Marnier. Pour sauce over the berries and garnish with puff pastry. Serve immediately. Makes 4 servings.

Alphonse Pignataro
MORGAN'S
Philadelphia, Pennsylvania

Resembling a delightful country inn, Morgan's in Philadelphia, Pennsylvania charms with pine wood booths and paneling, floral-patterned seat cushions in green, pink and orange tones and mixed fresh flower bouquets tucked in metal charlotte molds brightening the tables.

The menu itself is a work of art, illustrated with changing food graphics. Line drawings, some from seed catalogs of a century ago, some from baking company ads from the nineteen-twenties, some from vintage agricultural bulletins, add a whimsical touch.

Chef Alphonse Pignataro, 41, was a teacher of graphic arts, mechanical drawing and woodworking before he and his wife, Anita, decided to do what they had always dreamed of—open a restaurant.

At first they worked for others. They bought Morgan's in 1976 and completely restored the building. "It's a family business," says Pignataro. His wife runs the dining room, and he, the kitchen. Their four-year-old son has run of the premises.

Morgan's offers a French and Northern Italian menu interspersed with regional American specialties. Starters include fresh corn and crab chowder; sweetbread and oyster tart; poached scallops in a red pepper puree; and grilled venison sausage, served with pickled pears.

Entrées encompass sautéed softshell crabs with a shallot and pepper sauce; grilled quail glazed with cider honey vinegar; sautéed herb-breaded chicken breast with avocado sauce; and filet of beef with sauterne and Roquefort sauce.

"Desserts du Chariot," espresso and international coffees provide the finale.

A WINTER DINNER

Beet, Belgian Endive
and Feta Salad

Roast Squab Stuffed with
Sweetbreads and Vegetables

Hungarian Chocolate Cake

BEET, BELGIAN ENDIVE AND FETA SALAD

1 ½ pounds beets, tops
  removed (about 2 bunches)
6 tablespoons walnut oil
2 tablespoons tarragon vinegar
Salt and freshly ground black
  pepper to taste
3 bunches Belgian endive
¼ pound feta cheese
½ cup walnuts, toasted and
  coarsely chopped

Place beets in a shallow pan and bake in a 425°F. oven for 1 hour or until tender. Let cool, then peel and dice. Mix together the oil, vinegar, salt and pepper. Toss beets in half the vinaigrette. Arrange endive leaves in a spoke pattern on individual plates. Spoon beets in the center. Lightly dress endive with vinaigrette. Crumble feta over and scatter over the walnuts. Makes 6 servings.

NOTE If walnut oil is unavailable, use olive oil and 1 teaspoon Dijon-style mustard.

ROAST SQUAB STUFFED WITH SWEETBREADS AND VEGETABLES

6 squabs, dressed or Rock
  Cornish game hens
1 large onion, minced
3 carrots, peeled and minced
3 celery stalks, minced
3 tablespoons butter
1 pound veal Sweetbreads,
  blanched, peeled and broken
  into nuggets (page 148)
1 teaspoon fresh thyme or
  ¼ teaspoon dried thyme
Salt and freshly ground black
  pepper to taste
Sauce (following)

Wash squabs or game hens and pat dry. In a skillet sauté onion, carrots and celery in 2 tablespoons butter until tender and slightly browned. Let cool. Toss sweetbreads with the thyme and salt and pepper and mix in sautéed vegetables. Stuff cavities of birds loosely and truss. Brush birds with 1 tablespoon butter. Place on a rack in a roasting pan and roast in a 450°F. oven for 20 to 25 minutes or until golden brown. Serve Sauce alongside squab. Makes 6 servings.

SAUCE Reduce 1 ½ -2 cups Demi-Glace (page 148) until it coats the back of a spoon, add 2 finely chopped shallots and 1 teaspoon fresh thyme, and swirl in 3 tablespoons butter.

HUNGARIAN CHOCOLATE CAKE

2 eggs
2 cups buttermilk
2 cups all-purpose flour
2 ½ cups sugar
2 teaspoons baking soda
5 tablespoons sifted cocoa
  powder
½ cup Clarified Butter (page
  146)
1 cup whipping cream
Sugar and vanilla extract to
  taste
Chocolate Buttercream (page
  120 and omit praline)
Toasted slivered almonds for
  garnish
Chocolate shavings for garnish

In a large bowl with an electric mixer beat eggs and buttermilk thoroughly. Add flour and beat on medium speed several minutes. Add sugar and continue beating. Add soda, sifted cocoa and butter, mixing until smooth. Pour into two buttered and floured 9-inch cake pans. Bake in a 350°F. oven for 30 minutes or until a toothpick inserted comes out clean. Let cool on a rack.

To assemble cake, whip cream until stiff and sweeten with sugar and vanilla to taste. Spread cream between cake layers and on top of cake. Frost sides of cake with chocolate buttercream. Decorate sides with toasted slivered almonds and top with chocolate shavings. Chill well before serving. Makes 12 servings.

AN AUTUMN DINNER

Pheasant Terrine

Fish and Vegetable Stew

Pecan Tart

PHEASANT TERRINE

¾ pound pork fat
4 garlic cloves, minced
3 shallots, chopped
⅓ cup whipping cream
⅓ cup cognac or brandy
Pinch each allspice and ground cloves
1 teaspoon dried thyme
2 teaspoons salt
1 teaspoon freshly ground black pepper
½ cup all-purpose flour
4 eggs
1 ½ pounds ground veal
1 ½ pounds ground pork
1 ¼ pounds boned pheasant or chicken breast, finely diced
1 pound bacon
¾ pound pheasant or duck livers
4 bay leaves

In a food processor puree pork fat with garlic, shallots and cream. Mix in cognac, allspice, cloves, thyme, salt, pepper, flour and eggs. Gently mix in ground veal and pork and diced pheasant.

Line the bottom of a 9-by-5-inch loaf pan or terrine with strips of bacon. Place a layer of forcemeat in the bottom of the terrine, forming a well down the center of the pan. Set livers, closely packed, in the trough. Cover with remaining forcemeat. Cover top of terrine with bacon. Place bay leaves the length of terrine, and seal with foil. Set terrine in a baking pan and fill pan with hot water halfway up sides of mold. Bake in a 350°F. oven for 1 ½ hours or until cooked through. Weight and chill overnight before unmolding. Makes 16 servings.

FISH AND VEGETABLE STEW

2 medium onions, finely
  chopped
6 garlic cloves, minced
2 tablespoons corn or peanut
  oil
2 green bell peppers, minced
2 chili peppers, seeded and
  minced
3 cups dry white wine
2 cups Fish Stock (page 147)
2 cups finely diced yams
½ teaspoon crushed cumin
  seed
¼ teaspoon crushed saffron,
  soaked in 1 tablespoon water
3 bay leaves
Salt and freshly ground black
  pepper to taste
8 large tomatoes, peeled,
  seeded and chopped
3 pounds assorted seafood: red
  snapper, shark, lobster,
  shrimp, crab meat, sole,
  crayfish, oysters

In a large soup kettle sauté onion and garlic in oil until soft. Add green pepper and chili peppers and sauté 5 minutes. Add wine, fish stock, yams, cumin, saffron, bay leaves and salt and pepper. Bring to a boil and let simmer 10 minutes. Add tomatoes. Add cubed or sliced fish and shellfish and poach lightly, about 4 minutes. Serve in bowls. Makes 8 to 10 servings.

PECAN TART

10-inch baked Tart Shell (page
  150)
2 cups firmly packed brown
  sugar
3 tablespoons all-purpose flour
6 tablespoons whipping cream
3 eggs
1 tablespoon cider vinegar
1 teaspoon vanilla extract
2 tablespoons bourbon
¼ pound butter, melted
2 cups chopped pecans
1 ½ cups pecan halves
Whipped cream for garnish
  (optional)

Prepare the tart shell using a fluted flan pan with removable bottom. In a large bowl mix together the sugar and flour. Add cream and beat in eggs, one at a time. Mix in vinegar, vanilla, bourbon and butter. Fold in chopped nuts. Pour into the baked tart shell. Arrange pecan halves in concentric circles on top. Bake in a 325°F. oven for 40 to 45 minutes or until set and browned. Let cool on a rack. If desired, serve with lightly sweetened whipped cream. Makes 8 servings.

Michael Foley
PRINTER'S ROW
Chicago, Illinois

Michael Foley, a ruggedly handsome blond and bearded young chef of 30, opened Printer's Row restaurant in 1981 as part of the redevelopment of the south end of the Chicago Loop. The restaurant's name derived from its location in the old printing house district.

Its early American decor features dark wood paneling and soft tones of mauve, burgundy and gray. A generous liquor bar and a small wine bar serve the ninety seats.

Highly imaginative fare, borrowed from the cuisines of the world, comprises the menu. Foley says, "We consider the minorities of the area, the products in the locale and what's available within flying distance. Then we take the classics and adapt them to come up with something interesting but not trendy. It's a combination of cooking background and imagination."

Foley started working in his father and grandfather's "steak

and potatoes-style restaurant" known as Ray Foley's when he was twelve years old. The family operation was so successful that the Foleys later operated a Hyatt concession in Chicago with thirteen hundred seats.

Foley's early training was basically German with a little classical French, later augmented by working in small restaurants in New York,

Washington, D.C. and Europe, specifically France, Germany and Switzerland. He earned a B.A. in history from Georgetown University and completed graduate work at Cornell University's School of Hotel and Restaurant Administration.

A seasonal autumn menu at Printer's Row includes sliced homemade sausage with marinated pine nut salad, mussels steamed with tomato and basil, ragout of sweetbreads and kidneys in mustard, and smooth pâté of chicken livers with Gorgonzola cream.

Entrées may feature salmon finished with fresh oranges and mint, sautéed veal medallions with a light artichoke stew, venison sautéed with pomegranate juice and walnuts and medallions of beef tenderloin with ginger and vermouth.

For desserts, diners may find hazelnut pound cake with cinnamon cream, pear bavarian with ginger and pistachios, apple crumb tart with cranberry compote, lime custard with mint madeleines and a trio of homemade ice creams or sorbets served in a rippled praline cookie.

AN AUTUMN MENU

Grilled Brochette of Scallops with Oranges and Celery

Roast Quail Stuffed with Sweetbreads

Walnut Honey Pie

GRILLED BROCHETTE OF SCALLOPS WITH ORANGES AND CELERY

3 oranges
2 tablespoons celery leaves
1 teaspoon coarsely ground pepper
1 pound sea scallops
4 tablespoons unsalted butter

Peel and carefully segment 1 orange. Squeeze the juice from the remaining two oranges and place in a bowl. Add celery leaves, pepper and the scallops and marinate 30 minutes. Arrange scallops on skewers. Reserve marinade.

Grill scallops over medium-hot coals, or broil, cooking only until scallops are warm, but still slightly opaque inside, about 3 minutes.

Place marinade in a saucepan, bring to a boil, and reduce by half. Whisk in butter, one tablespoon at a time. Arrange scallop brochettes on individual plates and spoon over sauce. Garnish with orange segments. Makes 4 servings.

ROAST QUAIL STUFFED WITH SWEETBREADS

12 quail
Salt
4 ounces Sweetbreads, blanched, peeled and separated into nuggets (page 148)
Stock
5 tablespoons unsalted butter
2 cups whipping cream
1 teaspoon fresh minced thyme or tarragon or ¼ teaspoon dried thyme or tarragon
Garnish: 4 ounces enoki mushrooms;* white turnips, julienned and blanched; quartered blanched fresh artichoke hearts

Bone the quail removing all bones except the leg and thigh. Reserve bones for stock. Lightly season the inside with salt. Stuff each of the quail with an equal amount of the sweetbreads. With the quail bones make a light stock.

In a large skillet brown the birds in 1 tablespoon butter, turning them frequently until they are browned on all sides. Drain the pan. Add a rack to the pan and set the birds on the rack. Roast in a 350°F. oven, basting often with any accumulated pan juices, about 10 to 15 minutes or until the birds are plump and cooked almost until the juices run clear. Remove the birds to a platter and let rest.

Discard any fat from the roasting pan. Add the stock to the pan and reduce liquid until the stock is flavorful. Add cream and reduce until the liquid coats a spoon. Whip in remaining butter, 1 tablespoon at a time, and thyme or tarragon. To serve ladle a little of the sauce onto individual plates. Arrange two birds in the center of each plate, then garnish with mushrooms, turnips and artichoke hearts. Makes 6 servings.

Available at Oriental and specialty produce markets.

WALNUT HONEY PIE

10-inch Pastry Shell (following)
2 ¼ cups walnuts
1 cup sugar
¼ pound butter
1 teaspoon vanilla extract
1 tablespoon whipping cream
4 eggs, separated
3 tablespoons dark rum
Whipped cream or ice cream
  for garnish (optional)

First prepare Pastry Shell. For filling, place the nuts and sugar in a food processor and process until ground. Add butter, vanilla, cream and egg yolks and process again until mixed.

In a separate bowl beat the egg whites until soft peaks form. Fold one-third of the whites into the walnut mixture

to lighten it, then fold in remaining whites. Spread in the Pastry Shell. Bake in a 425°F. oven for 15 minutes. Reduce heat to 350°F. and continue baking 20 minutes longer. Let cool in pan on a rack. Remove pan sides, cut in wedges and garnish with whipped cream or ice cream. Makes 8 servings.

PASTRY SHELL Mix together 1 cup all-purpose flour, ½ cup butter and 2 tablespoons confectioners' sugar until crumbly. Pat into the bottom and sides of a 10-inch springform pan. Chill. Bake in a 425°F. oven for 5 minutes or until partially baked.

A WINTER MENU

Ravioli with Chèvre and Broccoli Cream

Roast Leg of Lamb with Walnuts and Pomegranates

Chocolate Mocha Roll with Sambucca Ice Cream

RAVIOLI WITH CHEVRE AND BROCCOLI CREAM

Pasta Dough (page 148) or
  wonton skins
¼ cup chopped leeks (white
  part only)
1 garlic clove, minced
4 tablespoons butter
1 tablespoon chopped parsley
3 ounces chèvre
Freshly ground pepper to taste
Egg Wash (1 egg beaten with 1
  tablespoon water)
Broccoli Cream (following)

Have pasta dough available or
use wonton skins. For stuffing,
in a small skillet sauté leek and
garlic in 2 tablespoons butter
until transparent. Add parsley.
Gently stir in chèvre. Season
with pepper. Let cool. Roll out
pasta dough thinly. With a ravioli cutter mark individual ravioli. Place a small spoonful of
stuffing on each marked circle
or square. Coat with egg wash
and place a second sheet on
top of the first. Press together.

Cut out ravioli. For wonton
skins, place a spoonful of stuffing on each skin. Brush edges
with egg wash and fold like an
envelope. Seal carefully.

Cook the ravioli in a large
pot of boiling salted water until
just tender, about 3 to 4 minutes. Drain well. Turn out on a
platter or individual plates and
spoon over the Broccoli Cream.
Makes 6 servings.

BROCCOLI CREAM Blanch 1 ½
cups broccoli flowerets in boiling salted water until just tender and drain well. Add 1 cup
strong Chicken Stock (page
147), a pinch of salt and freshly
ground nutmeg and 1 cup
whipping cream. Place mixture
in a blender and blend until
smooth. Turn into a saucepan,
add 2 tablespoons butter and
heat until hot through.

ROAST LEG OF LAMB WITH WALNUTS AND POMEGRANATES

1 leg of lamb (6 to 7 pounds),
  boned and tied
3 garlic cloves, peeled and
  slivered
Salt and freshly ground black
  pepper to taste
3 cups pomegranate juice
1 medium onion, cut in 1-inch
  pieces
6 tablespoons butter
¼ cup lightly roasted chopped
  walnuts
Accompaniments: roasted
  potatoes, butter-glazed
  scallions, spinach blanched
  and tossed in garlic butter

Make several small incisions in
lamb and insert small slivers of
garlic. Season with salt and
pepper. Place in a bowl, pour
pomegranate juice over and let
marinate overnight in the refrigerator, turning the roast
several times.

In a large skillet sauté onion
in 2 tablespoons butter until
limp. Transfer to a roasting
pan. Add lamb to skillet (reserve marinade) and sauté until
browned on all sides. Place
meat on top of onion in roast-

ing pan. Roast meat in a 425°F. oven for 20 minutes. Reduce temperature to 350°F. and continue roasting until meat thermometer registers 140°F. for rare or 145°F. for medium rare.

Transfer roast to a carving board. Skim fat from pan juices and deglaze pan drippings with the reserved marinade. Bring to a boil and scrape up drippings well. Reduce slightly to desired flavor. Strain. Return to saucepan and whip in remaining 4 tablespoons butter and the roasted walnuts.

Slice roast and add any accumulated juices to the finished sauce. Spoon sauce over meat. Spoon onto plates and accompany with roasted potatoes, butter-glazed scallions and spinach tossed in garlic butter. Makes about 8 servings.

CHOCOLATE MOCHA ROLL

⅓ cup strong coffee or espresso
6 ounces bittersweet or
  semisweet chocolate
½ cup sugar
6 eggs, separated
Confectioners' sugar
Mocha Buttercream (following)

Butter and flour a 10-by-15-inch jelly roll pan. In a double boiler place the coffee and chocolate and melt over warm water. Transfer to a mixing bowl. Stir in sugar and egg yolks, one at a time, and with an electric mixer beat at high speed until light and fluffy. In a separate bowl, with a clean beater, beat the egg whites until soft peaks form. Fold into the chocolate mixture. Turn into the prepared pan and bake in a 350°F. oven for 12 minutes, or until cake just leaves the sides of the pan. Do not overbake.

Turn out the cake on a tea towel lightly dusted with confectioners' sugar. Roll the cake when it has cooled just about to room temperature. When completely cool, unroll, spread with two-thirds of the Mocha Buttercream. Carefully roll up. Place on a serving platter and frost the outside of the cake with remaining buttercream. Slice and accompany with Sambucca Ice Cream. Makes 12 servings.

MOCHA BUTTERCREAM In a saucepan place ¾ cup strong espresso and ¾ cup sugar. Bring to a boil and boil for 2 minutes. In an electric mixer beat 6 egg yolks until light and fluffy. Stream in the coffee mixture and continue to beat until the mixture cools to room temperature. Add ¾ pound soft butter, one piece at a time, until blended in.

SAMBUCCA ICE CREAM

1 quart whole milk
12 egg yolks
2 cups sugar
2 teaspoons vanilla extract
2 cups whipping cream
¼ cup sambucca or other
  licorice-flavored liqueur

Scald the milk. In an electric mixer beat the egg yolks with sugar until light and fluffy. Stir in the hot milk. In a double boiler cook mixture over hot water until custard coats a spoon. Remove from heat and stir in vanilla. Mix in cream and chill. When ready to freeze, stir in sambucca. Churn in an ice cream freezer following manufacturer's instructions until frozen. Makes about 2 ½ quarts.

Barry Wine
THE QUILTED GIRAFFE
New York City, New York

New York attorney Barry Wine, 41, always wanted to own a restaurant. As a hobby he opened The Quilted Giraffe about nine years ago, in 1976. Within a year he was in the kitchen as a chef, leaving his law practice behind.

The elegant and expensive restaurant offers the best in ambience, service and food. Wood paneling, art deco glass, flowers, fine china and crystal set a mood of luxury that is underscored by the outstanding fare.

Late in 1984, the restaurant will move to an impressive new location, the world headquarters for AT&T, at 55th Street and Madison Avenue, designed by architect Philip Johnson.

Wine's interest in cooking was evident as a youngster in Milwaukee, Wisconsin. Both of his parents worked, and Wine prepared dinner for his family.

Wine modeled The Quilted Giraffe on what he, as a customer, would want, with an exciting menu and setting. The menu stems from his travels throughout the world.

Among the appetizers are wild mushroom soup with truffles, snail strudel, consommé with foie gras ravioli and caviar "beggar's purses." Notable entrées are rack of lamb with fennel and sour cherries, calves' liver with three nuts, rare breast of duck with turnips and lobster yakitori with sweet frites.

Desserts tempt with pecan squares, three little mousses, chocolate fudge cake, fresh ricotta with raspberries and cream and a hot fudge sundae with halvah.

AN AUTUMN DINNER

Snail Strudel

Scalloped Eggplant and
Potatoes with Garlic

Confit of Duck

Cranberry Sherbet

SNAIL STRUDEL

3 heads garlic, peeled
Peanut, corn or vegetable oil
1 medium-sized eggplant,
  peeled and diced
2 zucchini, diced
1 onion, diced
2 green peppers, seeded and
  diced
12 domestic mushrooms,
  thickly sliced
Olive oil
3 tomatoes, peeled, seeded and
  chopped
1 cup whipping cream
4 tablespoons butter
Salt and freshly ground black
  pepper to taste
Fresh lemon juice (about 1
  tablespoon)
2 cups canned snails or sea
  snails
Filo dough (about 12 sheets)
Melted butter

In a small saucepan, cover garlic with oil and cook over very low heat for 30 minutes. Let cool; reserve the oil to season other dishes or to cook more confit of garlic.

In a large sauté pan over high heat, separately cook the eggplant, zucchini, onion, peppers and mushrooms in olive oil. As each one is sautéed, turn into a strainer placed over a bowl and let the liquid drain. In the hot sauté pan, quickly toss the chopped tomato. Let any excess liquid evaporate. Add the tomatoes to the strainer.

Pour the collected liquid into a saucepan, whisk in the cream and the butter, one tablespoon at a time; boil while whisking for 2 minutes. Pour into a food processor or blender, add the confit of garlic and puree. Mix with the cooked vegetables and correct the seasoning with salt, pepper and lemon juice. Let cool. Drain the snails and add them to the vegetable mixture just before ready to roll the strudel.

Lay out a sheet of filo (keep remainder covered with plastic wrap or a towel), brush with melted butter, and cover with three more sheets of filo, buttering each sheet. Spoon a strip of filling along a long side of the filo, leaving a 1 ½ -inch border. Fold up sides 1 inch and roll up lengthwise. Place seam side down on a buttered baking sheet. Repeat with remaining filo and filling. Brush top with melted butter. Bake in a 375°F. oven for 15 to 20 minutes or until golden brown. Cut in slices. Makes 3 rolls, or about 12 servings.

SCALLOPED EGGPLANT AND POTATOES WITH GARLIC

8 domestic mushrooms, coarsely chopped
1 medium onion, chopped
7 garlic cloves, minced
3 sprigs fresh thyme or ¾ teaspoon dried thyme
1 tablespoon butter
½ cup water
4 tablespoons sherry wine vinegar
1 small eggplant, peeled and chopped
2 to 4 tablespoons olive oil
2 ounces pine nuts, toasted
Salt and freshly ground black pepper to taste
2 pounds boiling potatoes
1 cup whipping cream
1 cup milk

In a large skillet gently sauté the chopped mushrooms, onion, 3 cloves of the garlic and thyme in butter. Add the water and sherry wine vinegar and reduce over moderate heat until the mixture has a syrupy consistency. Let cool slightly and puree in a food processor or blender.

In a skillet sauté eggplant in oil over high heat until cooked through and slightly browned. Fold the eggplant chunks and pine nuts into the puree and correct the seasoning with salt and pepper.

Peel and slice potatoes ¼ -inch-thick, but do not wash again as starch is essential to this dish. In a large saucepan bring cream and milk to a simmer. Add the sliced potatoes, remaining garlic and salt and pepper to taste. Simmer 8 to 10 minutes, or until just tender.

Combine the potato mixture and the eggplant mixture in a buttered ovenproof casserole. Place casserole in baking pan filled with hot water halfway up the sides of the casserole and bake in a 375°F. oven until the top is nicely browned, about 30 minutes. Makes 8 servings.

CONFIT OF DUCK*

1 duck (5 pounds)
6 garlic cloves
2 teaspoons salt
Rendered duck fat**

Cut the duck into four pieces: two leg and thigh sections and two breasts. Leave the breasts on the bone so they retain their shape, but bone the legs and thighs. Place the duck pieces, garlic, salt and enough rendered fat to cover the pieces in a small flameproof casserole. Heat until the fat just begins to bubble. Reduce heat to low and simmer, covered, 1 hour and 45 minutes or until the meat feels very tender.

Carefully remove duck pieces to a pan. Cover and refrigerate 1 hour. Remove breast meat from the bone and scrape away excess fat and jagged edges of skin. Heat a small amount of oil or duck grease in a skillet until almost smoking. Place duck pieces skin side down in the skillet and brown them about 5 minutes; do not turn. Cover skillet. Bake in a 400°F. oven for 7 minutes. Makes 6 servings.

*Confit is generally referred to as the preserved meat of duck, goose, or pork, which after cooking is covered with its own fat. The same idea is done here with garlic.

**Rendered duck fat from a roasted duck can be frozen for later use.

CRANBERRY SHERBET

2 packages (12 ounces each)
  fresh or frozen cranberries
  (thawed, if frozen)
¾ cup sugar
1 cup water
1 cup apple cider
Zest of 1 orange
Pinch salt
¼ cup gin
1 ½ tablespoons fresh lemon
  juice

In a saucepan combine the
cranberries, sugar, water, apple
cider, orange zest and salt.
Bring to a boil and let simmer 3
to 4 minutes or until all the
cranberries have popped. Let
cool slightly, pour into a
blender or food processor and
puree. Strain, discarding the
pulp. Add gin and lemon juice
to the cranberry mixture. Chill.
Churn in an ice cream freezer
following manufacturer's instructions until frozen. Makes
about 1 ½ quarts.

A SPRING MENU

Risotto with Smoked Salmon

Saddle of Lamb with Fennel
and Pickled Cherries

Chocolate Fudge Cake

RISOTTO WITH SMOKED SALMON

1 pound salmon fillet
Salt and freshly ground black
  pepper to taste
¼ cup wild rice
½ cup water
1 cup Chicken Stock (page 147)
½ celery root or 2 stalks celery,
  chopped
4 shallots, diced
¾ cup white rice
Salt and freshly ground black
  pepper to taste
1 cup milk
½ cup whipping cream
1 teaspoon wasabi (Japanese
  powdered green horseradish
  root)*
1 bunch scallions, chopped

Use a smoker fueled with mesquite or hickory chips to smoke
the salmon. Season the salmon
with salt and pepper. Smoke
fish in moderate heat until just
barely cooked in the center. Let
cool. If preferred, substitute
commercial smoked salmon.

In a small saucepan combine
wild rice and water and simmer, covered, until tender,
about 45 minutes. In another
saucepan bring chicken stock
to a boil, add celery root, shallots, white rice and salt and
pepper and simmer until most
of the liquid has evaporated.

Heat milk and cream until
steaming, pour into the rice pot
and continue simmering until
mixture is a thick liquid, but
not pasty. Stir in wild rice and
the wasabi. Season with salt
and pepper. Break the salmon
by hand along its natural divi-
sions into attractive pieces.
When ready to serve, reheat
the rice (risotto) and transfer to
a serving platter or individual
plates. Arrange salmon on top.
Sprinkle with scallions. Makes
4 servings.

Available at Japanese markets.

SADDLE OF LAMB WITH FENNEL AND PICKLED CHERRIES

1 small loin of lamb (about 4 to 4 ½ pounds), boned and trimmed
Butter and vegetable oil
1 ½ cups Lamb Stock (page 147)
2 tablespoons vinegar from jar of pickled wild cherries or raspberry vinegar
2 bulbs fennel, trimmed, julienned and blanched
8 ounces pickled wild cherries, or brandied cherries mixed with 3 tablespoons raspberry vinegar
4 tablespoons unsalted butter
Salt and freshly ground black pepper to taste

In a large skillet sauté the lamb in a little butter and oil, turning it until browned and cooking just until quite rare. Let rest in a warm place. Degrease the pan, add the stock, vinegar, fennel and pickled cherries and reduce the mixture for 1 minute. Whisk in the butter, one tablespoon at a time. Season with salt and pepper. Slice the meat into ¼-inch-thick slices and arrange on individual plates. Nap the slices with the sauce. Makes 4 to 6 servings.

CHOCOLATE FUDGE CAKE

9 ounces bittersweet or semisweet chocolate
7 tablespoons unsalted butter
6 eggs, separated
2 egg whites
1 tablespoon cognac or Armagnac
Pinch salt
½ cup lukewarm water
Unsweetened whipped cream for garnish

In a double boiler over hot water melt chocolate and butter. Place egg yolks and the 8 whites in separate mixing bowls and let warm to room temperature. Beat the yolks until light in color, mix in the cognac, and blend into the melted chocolate mixture. Add salt and stir in the lukewarm water.

Beat the egg whites until soft peaks form and fold carefully into the chocolate mixture. Turn into a buttered, floured 9-inch springform pan. Bake in a 325°F. oven for about 20 minutes, or until the center of the cake is barely set. Let cool, remove from pan and serve with whipped cream. Makes 10 servings.

Richard Perry
RICHARD PERRY
RESTAURANT
St. Louis, Missouri

The Richard Perry Restaurant is located in a typically narrow south St. Louis structure which was built in 1897 as a tavern. It served that function through Prohibition when it was a well-known speakeasy. Later it became a confectionery.

In January, 1972, proprietor Richard Perry opened the Jefferson Avenue Boarding House at this location, serving food based on authentic recipes from old St. Louis's finest hotels, restaurants, riverboats and homes. On the restaurant's tenth anniversary, Perry changed its name to his to reflect a new image and a change of service. Instead of a fixed menu, diners now have a choice of dishes from a selection of Perry's own creations. In addition to dinner, luncheon and Sunday brunch are served as well.

The interior retains a turn-of-the-century flavor with dark wood paneling, brown walls and cork ceiling. Pink or red rosebuds adorn the tables.

Specialties from chef Richard Perry, 45, include egg pasta with duck meat and fresh figs, baked mushrooms stuffed three ways, seafood sausage with two sauces, braised veal shanks with morels, and salmon fillet breaded in pine nuts sauté. Side dishes include grated zucchini sauté with onion butter, old-fashioned corn custard and fresh asparagus with puff pastry.

Perry grew up on a farm in Illinois. While his father served in World War II, Perry was pressed into extra service at home, including helping his mother cook. He graduated from the University of Illinois, specializing in history, and worked for McGraw-Hill in New York and Chicago. Then an amateur cook, he claims "temporary insanity" when he launched his restaurant business twelve years ago. "Had I known what I know now, I wouldn't have done it, but I wouldn't trade it," he vows.

A SPRING DINNER

Seviche of Blue Gill

Sea Scallops Sauté
with Pink Butter

Rhubarb Bavarian with
Strawberry Sauce

SEVICHE OF BLUE GILL

¾ pound blue gill fillets
1 pimiento, seeded and
  chopped
1 green pepper, seeded and
  chopped
¼ cup lime juice
¼ cup water
2 tablespoons extra virgin olive
  oil
¼ cup minced fresh parsley
2 tablespoons minced shallots
2 garlic cloves, minced
½ teaspoon salt
¼ teaspoon Tabasco sauce
1 ½ teaspoons chopped fresh
  oregano or ½ teaspoon dried
  oregano
Butter lettuce or other greens
1 lime, cut in wedges for
  garnish

Cut fish into bite-sized chunks and place in a bowl with peppers, lime juice, water, oil, parsley, shallots, garlic, salt, Tabasco and oregano. Stir well. Cover and refrigerate 6 hours or overnight.

Arrange greens on 4 salad plates and spoon over the seviche. Garnish with lime wedges. Makes 4 servings.

SEA SCALLOPS SAUTE WITH PINK BUTTER

2 cups juice from blood
  oranges or regular oranges*
2 cups blanc de noir sparkling
  wine, or champagne
¼ cup champagne vinegar
1 shallot, chopped
¼ teaspoon salt
¼ teaspoon white pepper
½ to ¾ pound unsalted butter,
  cut in pieces
1 pound sea scallops
2 tablespoons unsalted butter
4 hot Puff Pastry shells (page
  149)

In a saucepan combine 1 ½ cups of the orange juice, wine, vinegar, shallot, salt and pepper. Bring to a boil and reduce to a thick glaze. Add the remaining ½ cup orange juice and whisk in the butter, one piece at a time, making a creamy sauce.

In a skillet sauté scallops very quickly in about 2 tablespoons butter. To serve, divide the scallops among the 4 pastry shells and spoon over each with the butter sauce. Makes 4 servings.

Only blood orange juice will tint butter pink.

RHUBARB BAVARIAN WITH STRAWBERRY SAUCE

Rhubarb Puree (following)
2 egg yolks
¼ cup sugar
½ cup milk
1 ½ teaspoons unflavored
  gelatin
1 ½ tablespoons cold water
1 cup whipping cream
Strawberry Sauce (following)

Prepare Rhubarb Puree. For bavarian, beat egg yolks until thick and light in color and beat in sugar. Scald milk and stir in. In a double boiler, cook over hot water, stirring, until custard coats a spoon. Soften gelatin in cold water. Stir in the softened gelatin, stirring until it is completely incorporated. Let cool until almost set. Fold in Rhubarb Puree. Whip cream until stiff and fold in. Spoon into individual molds, about 6 ounce capacity. Refrigerate until firm. To serve, unmold by dipping in a pan of hot water; turn out on dessert plates and surround with Strawberry Sauce. Makes 6 to 8 servings.

RHUBARB PUREE Dice ¼ pound rhubarb. In a saucepan combine rhubarb with ½ cup water and 3 tablespoons sugar; cover and cook until tender, about 10 minutes. Puree in a food processor or blender. Stir in 1 teaspoon lemon juice and 2 teaspoons Cointreau.

STRAWBERRY SAUCE Slice 2 cups strawberries thinly and place in a bowl with ¼ cup sugar and ¼ cup Triple Sec or other orange-flavored liqueur. Let macerate 2 hours or longer. Puree in a food processor or blender. Makes 2 cups sauce.

A WINTER MENU

Creamed Oysters and
Mushrooms

Veal Shanks with Morels

Apricot Bavarian with
Raspberry Sauce

CREAMED OYSTERS AND MUSHROOMS

2 shallots, chopped
½ cup dry white wine
¼ cup Fish Stock (page 147)
1 ½ cups whipping cream
20 oysters, shucked
1 cup mushrooms, sliced
2 tablespoons dry sherry
2 teaspoons fresh lemon juice
¼ cup chopped green onions
Salt and white pepper to taste
Puff Pastry crescents (page 149)

In a saucepan combine the shallots, wine, and stock and reduce to ¼ cup liquid; set aside. In another saucepan reduce the cream to 1 cup. Add the shallot reduction, the oysters, mushrooms, sherry and lemon juice. Continue to reduce until the sauce is thick. Stir in green onions. Season with salt and pepper. Serve on individual plates with puff pastry crescents. Makes 4 servings.

VEAL SHANKS WITH MORELS

6 veal shanks with marrow, cut in 2-inch pieces (about 4 pounds)
Salt and freshly ground black pepper to taste
1 tablespoon olive oil
¼ cup chopped leeks (white part only)
¼ cup chopped carrots
¼ cup chopped celery
1 cup dry white wine
½ cup Chicken Stock (page 147)
¼ cup Beef or Veal Stock (page 147)
¼ cup chopped fresh or canned plum tomatoes, peeled, seeded and drained
3 sprigs parsley
1 bay leaf
1 teaspoon chopped fresh thyme or ¼ teaspoon dried thyme
1 cup whipping cream
¼ cup morel mushrooms, chopped, or 1 ounce dried mushrooms reconstituted in ¼ cup warm water and chopped

Sprinkle veal shanks with salt and pepper. In a large skillet brown meat in oil on all sides. Transfer meat to a baking pan. Place leeks, carrots and celery in the skillet with wine and simmer 15 minutes. Add chicken stock and beef or veal stock, tomatoes, parsley, bay leaf and thyme and simmer 5 minutes longer. Pour over shanks, cover with foil and bake in a 350°F. oven for 1 ½ hours or until fork tender.

Transfer meat to a platter and keep warm. Strain sauce and reduce by half. Add cream and reduce until sauce is thickened. Add mushrooms and heat through. Spoon sauce onto each plate and place a shank on top. Serve with a small spoon for the marrow. Makes 6 servings.

APRICOT BAVARIAN WITH RASPBERRY SAUCE

2 egg yolks
¼ cup sugar
½ cup milk
1 ½ teaspoons unflavored gelatin
1 tablespoon cold water
4 ounces dried apricots
¼ cup water
1 tablespoon apricot brandy
2 tablespoons apricot preserves
1 cup whipping cream
Raspberry Sauce (following)

Beat egg yolks and sugar until thick and light in color. Scald milk and stir in. Place in a double boiler and cook over hot water, stirring, until custard coats a spoon. Soften gelatin in cold water, stir into the custard and stir until gelatin dissolves.

In a food processor or blender puree the apricots with water, brandy and preserves. Stir into the custard mixture. Whip cream until stiff and fold in. Spoon into individual molds, about 6 ounce size, or one large mold or soufflé dish. Cover and refrigerate until firm, about 2 hours. To unmold dip molds in hot water and turn out on dessert plates. Spoon about ¼ cup Raspberry Sauce around each mold. Makes 6 to 8 servings.

RASPBERRY SAUCE Puree 1 ½ cups raspberries in a food processor or blender and press through a sieve to discard seeds. Stir in 2 tablespoons sugar, 2 teaspoons fresh lemon juice and 2 tablespoons black currant liqueur.

Robert Rosellini
ROSELLINI'S OTHER PLACE
Seattle, Washington

Robert Rosellini, 38, the owner of Rosellini's Other Place in Seattle, Washington, is a fourth-generation restaurateur. "It was almost genetic to become a chef," he says.

From the age of ten or twelve he worked in the kitchen of his

father's restaurant in Seattle. (His Italian grandmother had first trained him.) Yet Rosellini headed in another career direction after school with degrees in marine transportation and meteorology from the U.S. Merchant Academy in Kings Point, New York, and two years of travel with the Merchant Marine.

"Then a dinner at Troisgros in France propelled me into the restaurant business. Never in my life had I experienced anything as magnificent as that dinner," Rosellini recalls. He stayed on in Europe to find out how he could recreate that experience.

His three-month vacation turned into a five-year stay as he tried out "a gambit of things—butchering, wine brokering and working in a slaughterhouse, game farm and trout farm, plus apprenticing with top chefs like Jacques Lascombe at the Lyon d'Or in Colony, near Geneva, Switzerland."

Inspired, Rosellini returned to Seattle and opened Rosellini's Other Place within six months. That was 1973.

The soft beige-toned dining room is accented with mirrors. Deep green banquettes provide seating. Changing flowers ornament the tables. "All the entertainment is on the plate," says Rosellini.

He has defined ten culinary seasons in the Pacific Northwest which he describes as a moment or interval of time when there is enough movement of a new product to change the menu. "The menu is a moving image of the area where I am living," he explains. "Naturally there are more seasons in summer as everything converges, than in winter."

Rosellini has played a key role in making produce available in his area that was scarce or nonexistent. He was aware of what was being overlooked, like salsify and squashes, and he provided interested growers with seeds that he or friends brought back from France, Italy and Belgium. "Now there is considerable winter farming where none existed before," he says.

A sampling of appetizers from Rosellini's Other Place includes pheasant liver pâté, warm cured lamb salad, cured sable and salmon with herbs, baked goat cheese with walnuts and steamed Penn Cove mussels. Entrées feature roast veal medallions with royal anne cherries and sage, broiled quillback rockfish with sorrel butter, roast pheasant with raspberries and pine nuts and roast nalgai antelope with red currants, marrow and burgundy. Sorbets and ices provide a palate cleanser between courses.

AN AUTUMN DINNER

Pheasant with Walnut and Cream Cheese Sauce

Pilaf

Herbed Green Beans

Apple-Basil Sorbet

Hazelnut Torte

PHEASANT WITH WALNUT AND CREAM CHEESE SAUCE

6 small pheasants (about 1 ½ pounds each) or Rock Cornish game hens
Salt and freshly ground black pepper to taste
Salt pork slices (about 3 ounces)
1 cup water
Bouquet garni (3 sprigs fresh parsley, 1 bay leaf, 2 sprigs fresh thyme or ½ teaspoon dried thyme, in a cheesecloth bag)
1 leek, chopped
1 carrot, chopped
½ cup port
4 ounces salt pork, julienned
12 ounces natural cream cheese
1 cup walnuts, toasted and chopped
½ teaspoon freshly ground black pepper and salt to taste

Reserve giblets, neck and wing tips of pheasants for sauce stock. Season the pheasants with salt and pepper inside and out. Truss, then place sliced salt pork over the breasts. Place on a rack in a roasting pan and roast in a 350°F. oven for 1 hour. Remove salt pork.

For sauce, place giblets, neck and wing tips in a saucepan with water, bouquet garni, leek and carrot. Bring to a boil, cover and simmer 30 minutes. Strain and reduce to ½ cup. Add the wine and heat until simmering. Fry the salt pork until crispy; drain and keep warm. In a mixing bowl beat the cream cheese until fluffy. Gradually beat in the warm stock and wine mixture, beating until smooth. Mix in sautéed salt pork, walnuts, and pepper and salt.

To serve, cut birds in half, if desired. Place birds on a platter and spoon over the sauce. Makes 6 or more servings.

APPLE-BASIL SORBET

6 tart cooking apples, peeled,
  cored and diced
1 quart apple juice
½ cup loosely packed fresh
  basil leaves, minced
Sugar to taste

In a saucepan cook apples with apple juice until the apples are soft. Let cool slightly, then puree in a blender or food processor. Cool and stir in basil. Freeze in an ice cream maker following manufacturer's instructions until frozen or half freeze in ice cube trays, then whip in a food processor until frothy and refreeze until firm. Makes about 1 ¼ quarts.

HAZELNUT TORTE

6 eggs
1 cup sugar
½ cup all-purpose flour
½ cup cocoa powder, sifted
½ cup finely chopped
  hazelnuts
½ cup Clarified Butter, cooled
  (page 146)
Chocolate Hazelnut
  Buttercream (following)
Toasted hazelnuts for garnish

In a mixing bowl beat eggs until thick and light in color and gradually beat in the sugar. Sift flour with the cocoa and fold into the eggs in three parts. Fold in hazelnuts and butter. Turn into a greased and floured 10-inch springform pan. Bake in a 350°F. oven for 30 to 35 minutes or until the cake springs back when lightly touched in the center. Loosen sides and bottom and turn out on a rack. Cool. Cut the cake into three horizontal layers and frost between layers and on top and sides with Chocolate Hazelnut Buttercream. Garnish with toasted hazelnuts. Makes 16 servings.

CHOCOLATE HAZELNUT BUTTER-CREAM In a saucepan over moderate heat, heat ⅓ cup sugar until it melts and caramelizes. Immediately turn out onto a greased cookie sheet; let stand until it hardens and cools. Break into small pieces. Grind in the food processor with ¼ cup toasted hazelnuts until a fine powder. Set aside. Boil 1 cup sugar and ½ cup water until it reaches 238°F. (soft ball stage) on a candy thermometer. With an electric mixer beat 6 egg yolks until thick and light and immediately beat in the hot sugar syrup. Continue beating until thick and fluffy and mixture cools to room temperature. Gradually beat in 10 ounces softened unsalted butter, two tablespoons at a time. Melt 3 ounces semisweet chocolate and stir in. Fold in the hazelnut praline.

A SUMMER MENU

Salad of Wild Greens and Herbs

Broiled Salmon with Sorrel

Yellow Crookneck and Zucchini Squash

Green Grape Sorbet

SALAD OF WILD GREENS AND HERBS

Compose a salad of well-washed, crisped leaves of lamb's quarters, anise hissop, narcissus, nasturtium blossoms, purslane, golden corn salad, chick weed, cress, borage, wild chrysanthemum leaves, shepherd's purse, peppermint and spearmint. Serve with a dressing composed of red currant vinegar blended with blackberry vinegar and extra virgin olive oil.

NOTE These are mostly wild greens and herbs. If none are available consider garden mints, nasturtium and cress.

BROILED SALMON WITH SORREL

¼ cup white wine vinegar
4 shallots, minced
¼ cup fresh lemon juice
¾ pound butter, cut into pieces
½ cup fresh sorrel, julienned
6 salmon fillets or steaks (6
 ounces each)
Olive oil
Salt and freshly ground black
 pepper to taste
Julienned sorrel for garnish

In a saucepan simmer the vinegar, shallots, and lemon juice until the liquid is reduced to 1 tablespoon. Over very low heat, whisk in the butter, one piece at a time. Strain and keep warm over low heat. Stir in the ½ cup julienned sorrel.

Meanwhile brush salmon with oil and season with salt and pepper. Broil or grill salmon just until it separates at its natural seams, about 4 to 5 minutes on each side. Spoon sauce on serving plates and top with broiled salmon. Garnish with julienned sorrel. Makes 6 servings.

GREEN GRAPE SORBET

3 pounds green grapes,
 stemmed and mashed
½ cup sugar

Cook the grapes with sugar until pulpy. Press through a food mill. Chill. Churn in an ice cream freezer following manufacturer's instructions until frozen or half freeze in ice cube trays, then whip until frothy in a food processor and return to the freezer until firm. Makes about 1 quart.

Cindy Black
SHEPPARD'S
Sheraton Harbor Island East
San Diego, California

Petite Cindy Black, 27, wears the head chef toque at Sheppard's, an elegant restaurant in San Diego overlooking a marina.

With poise and sparkle, Black commands a crew of ten, setting forth her interpretation of West Coast regional cuisine. It's drawn on her love for the French southwest and a curiosity about international fare.

A Wellesley graduate in French literature, Black grew up in a food-loving family. Her father, a foreign service diplomat, was her first mentor as she watched him prepare French gourmet dishes and pastries from a great black book of recipes.

Following graduation she enrolled in the professional chefs program at Madeline Kamman's Modern Gourmet Cooking School. Then she went abroad to perfect her culinary skills at Le Cabanon, a one-star restaurant in the Landes region of southwest France. Working from ten in the morning until midnight seven days a week, she excelled in preparing the local specialties—confits of duck and geese and fresh foie gras. She returned to Boston and worked up the ranks at Apley's, then moved on to become chef at The Cranberry Moose before opening Sheppard's for Sheraton on the West Coast.

Black acts as the "barker" or expediter, calling the orders to everyone on the line and arranging the timing.

Sheppard's small personalized menu offers eight to ten first courses and entrées plus five desserts. Specialties include grilled oysters with lime butter, lobster dumplings and smoked carpaccio. Entrées encompass duckling with pear brandy, venison with fresh currants and petrale sole in sage butter cream. Homemade Belgian chocolate ice cream and amaretto almond soufflé are outstanding desserts.

The restaurant is luxurious with warm apricot tones accented by lush protea flowers and orchid sprays spilling from Orrefors crystal vases on each table.

An unusual glass wine case housing nine hundred bottles, and a tiled display kitchen for whipping up dessert soufflés, lend interest. The soft, intimate decor is accented by original oil paintings with a French impressionist feeling and a blond wood buffet holds baskets of flowers and whimsical wooden hens. Soft harp music is a further pleasure.

A SUMMER MENU

Grilled Puget Sound Oysters with Lime Butter Sauce

Roast Squab with Tarragon

Glacéed Pear Ice Cream

GRILLED
PUGET SOUND OYSTERS
WITH LIME BUTTER SAUCE

16 Puget Sound oysters, freshly opened
Lime Butter Sauce (following)
Caviar for garnish
Lime wedges for garnish

Arrange the oysters on a baking pan and spoon over about 3 ounces Lime Butter Sauce per person or for four oysters. Bake in a 375°F. oven for 6 minutes or until hot through. Arrange four oysters on each plate and garnish with caviar and lime wedges. Makes 4 servings.

LIME BUTTER SAUCE In a saucepan combine 1 cup white wine, ½ cup lime juice, 1 tablespoon minced garlic, 2 tablespoons chopped shallots, 2 tablespoons Chinese bottled oyster sauce and 1 tablespoon chopped ginger root. Bring to a boil and reduce liquid to ¼ cup. Whisk in ½ pound softened unsalted butter, in pieces, one at a time. Finish with 3 to 4 tablespoons whipping cream and salt and white pepper to taste.

ROAST SQUAB WITH TARRAGON

4 whole fresh squab, each
  stuffed with a sprig of fresh
  tarragon or tarragon in
  vinegar
Salt and white pepper to taste
2 tablespoons butter
4 tablespoons cognac
Braised endive for
  accompaniment

Season squabs with salt and
pepper and sauté in butter in a
large skillet until golden
brown. Cover pan and cook
slowly until birds release their
juices. The legs will be tender
and the breast should be
slightly pink.
   Remove birds from pan and
clip in half. If desired, remove
rib cage. Skim fat from pan
juices and reduce juices
slightly. Return squab to the
pan and flame in cognac. Serve
with braised endive and cooking juices. Makes 4 servings.

GLACEED PEAR ICE CREAM

6 ripe pears, peeled and sliced
1 cup sugar
1 cup whipping cream
½ cup Stirred Custard
  (following)
½ cup Glacéed Pears
  (following)
¼ cup Pear William

Place the sliced pears in a buttered dish and sprinkle with
sugar. Bake in a 375°F. oven for
20 minutes or unitl the pears
are very caramelized. Deglaze
the baking dish with cream and
¼ cup liqueur. Let cool. Puree
the deglazed mixture and the
pears in a food processor or
blender. Add the ½ cup Stirred
Custard and Glacéed Pears.
Churn in an ice cream freezer
following manufacturer's instructions until frozen. Serve
ice cream with Stirred Custard
Sauce and slivers of Glacéed
Pears. Sprinkle Pear William
over the top. Makes 6 servings.

STIRRED CUSTARD Beat 4 egg
yolks with ½ cup sugar until
pale and creamy. Scald 1 cup
half-and-half and stir in. Place
in a double boiler and cook
over hot water until custard
coats a spoon . Stir in 1 tablespoon vanilla extract.

GLACEED PEARS Cook ¾ cup
dried pears in heavy sugar
syrup until plumped, about 15
minutes. Cool, then soak in 3
tablespoons Pear William.

A FALL MENU

Smoked Carpaccio

Red Snapper with Peppers
and Garlic Mayonnaise

Warm Almond Flan

SMOKED CARPACCIO

Soy-Ginger Marinade
  (following)
8 ounces beef tenderloin
2 tablespoons chopped shallots
2 tablespoons coarse-grain
  mustard
2 egg yolks
3 tablespoons balsamic vinegar
1 cup corn oil
3 tablespoons chopped fresh
  tarragon
¼ cup half-and-half
Salt and freshly ground black
  pepper to taste
Garnishes: cornichons, lemon
  wedges and capers

Prepare Soy-Ginger Marinade. Marinate beef in sauce, refrigerated, for 2 days. Remove meat from marinade and pat dry. Slowly smoke in a smoker for 2 hours. Chill. Just before serving, slightly freeze the meat; slice paper thin. To serve arrange several overlapping meat slices on each plate. Whisk together the shallots, mustard, egg yolks and vinegar in a small bowl. Slowly add oil to create a mayonnaise. Stir in tarragon, cream, and salt and pepper. Spoon sauce over the meat. Garnish with pickles, lemon wedges and capers. Makes 4 servings.

SOY-GINGER MARINADE Stir together ¾ cup soy sauce, ¼ cup red wine, 1 tablespoon minced garlic, 2 tablespoons chopped ginger root and ½ red onion, sliced.

RED SNAPPER WITH PEPPERS AND GARLIC MAYONNAISE

1 red onion, chopped
2 tablespoons minced garlic
2 sweet red peppers, seeded
  and coarsely chopped
2 ripe tomatoes, chopped or 1
  cup canned tomatoes
½ cup olive oil
½ cup white wine
1 bay leaf
1 sprig thyme
2 cups Fish Stock (page 146) or
  mussel juices
Salt and freshly ground black
  pepper to taste
2 tablespoons fresh lemon juice
4 red snapper fillets (about 7
  ounces each)
12 fresh mussels
Garlic Mayonnaise (following)

In a large skillet sauté onion, garlic, peppers and tomatoes in olive oil. Add wine, bay leaf and thyme. Reduce liquid by one-half. Add fish stock. Cover and simmer about 45 minutes or until a rich flavor develops. Uncover and reduce liquid to about 2 cups. Let cool slightly and puree liquid and vegetables in a food processor or blender. Season with salt and pepper. Add lemon juice.

  Heat fish in sauce, cooking just until tender, about 6 minutes. Add mussels and cook just until opened, about 2 minutes. Arrange snapper pieces on individual plates and top with sauce and Garlic Mayonnaise. Makes 4 servings.

GARLIC MAYONNAISE Puree in a food processor or blender or whisk together until creamy 2 egg yolks, ¼ cup fresh lemon juice, 2 tablespoons minced garlic, ½ cup chopped fresh parsley, 1 slice bread, chopped, ½ teaspoon paprika, ¼ teaspoon cayenne pepper and 1 tablespoon tomato paste. Slowly add 1 cup olive oil. Season with salt and freshly ground black pepper to taste. Thin with braising liquid, if desired.

WARM ALMOND FLAN

3 eggs
½ cup sugar
1 cup toasted chopped
  almonds
8 ounces almond paste, cut in
  ¼ -inch cubes
½ teaspoon vanilla extract
1 cup whipping cream
1 cup milk
2 tablespoons apricot brandy or
  other liqueur
9-inch baked Pastry Shell (page
  150)
3 tablespoons sugared sliced
  almonds
Whipped cream for garnish

Whisk eggs together with sugar and stir in toasted almonds, almond paste and vanilla. Add cream, milk and brandy. Turn into the pastry shell. Bake in a 325°F. oven for 20 minutes; sprinkle the top with sugared sliced almonds and bake 10 minutes longer or until set. Let cool slightly, cut in wedges and serve with whipped cream. Makes 8 servings.

Christian Iser
Jim Dodge
STANFORD COURT HOTEL
San Francisco, California

Together executive chef Christian Iser and pastry chef Jim Dodge are developing their own style at the elegant Stanford Court Hotel on top of Nob Hill.

This talented team directs a staff of forty-five serving six hundred restaurant meals a day for two restaurants: Fournou's Ovens and Cafe Potpourri. Banquet menus can raise the tally to one thousand.

They make whatever the hotel needs—Beaujolais vinegar, flavored pasta, sauces and pastries, tray after tray of butter cookies, praline sticks, truffles and chocolate filigrees (secured in a padlocked box to minimize unofficial sampling).

Growing up in the Cognac region of France, Iser always wanted to be a chef, though there were none in his family. At fifteen he apprenticed in Paris and trained at the Jean Drouant School. Later he

Christian Iser

Jim Dodge

127

worked in a small French restaurant in New York. When he came to San Francisco in 1972 he landed a job at the Stanford Court his first day in the city. His favorite station is garde manger, involving cold food decoration and ice carving.

Dodge apprenticed at his family's resort, The Inn at Steel Hill in Sanborton, New Hampshire, at a Swiss pastry shop, Strawberry Court, and at resorts on Mackinac Island and in Florida. After only one day with a huge San Francisco hotel chain, Dodge left and has been at the Stanford Court the past six years.

Dodge is a master pastry maker. Gorgeous brioche, puff pastry, tiny, uniform petit four sec and an eight-layer Chocolate Beret Cake are prepared with deceptive ease. His most popular dessert is Praline Ice Cream Pie with Rum Sauce.

Dodge shares his talents at cooking classes in private San Francisco cooking schools. "Teaching is a love and a good insight into our clientele," he explains. It is a way to find out what is appealing to customers. "It also helps when I teach my staff. I realize you have to be very thorough, like a home cook."

From the exceptional wood and gas-fired tile oven in the spacious dining room at Fournou's Ovens comes rack of lamb, the most favored entrée of the patrons. Other specialties include terrine of fresh duck liver with pistachios, smoked salmon trout with sour cream and cucumbers, bay shrimp and melon and crab bisque for starters.

Seasonally available seafood includes sea bass baked in orange butter, sole with brown-buttered filberts, or cumin-spiced snapper with lime and fresh coriander. Duckling with green peppercorns and kumquat sauce and piccata of veal with lemon are standouts among the entrées.

A SPRING DINNER

Salad à la Grecque

Medallions of Veal with Chive Cream Sauce

Asparagus and New Potatoes

Praline Ice Cream Pie

SALAD A LA GRECQUE

1 cup red wine vinegar
1 cup olive oil
1 cup dry white wine
4 to 6 ounces shiitake
    mushrooms, quartered
16 pitted green olives
2 dozen Kalamata (Greek)
    olives
2 dozen large peeled whole
    garlic cloves

1 dozen large peeled whole
  shallots
2 teaspoons chopped fresh
  tarragon or ½ teaspoon dried
  tarragon
¼ teaspoon salt
Butter lettuce cups
3 green onions, cut in 2-inch
  lengths for garnish
Parsley sprigs for garnish
4 lemon halves, cut like flowers
  and sprinkled with parsley
  and paprika for garnish
Carrot slivers for garnish

In a skillet reduce the vinegar,
oil and wine by one-half, cooking until caramel-colored. Add
the mushrooms, green olives,
Kalamata olives, garlic, shallots, tarragon and salt and simmer until ½ cup of liquid remains. Let cool. To serve,
spoon into lettuce cups and
garnish with green onions,
parsley and lemon flowers.
Scatter over carrot slivers.
Makes 4 first course servings.

MEDALLIONS OF VEAL WITH CHIVE CREAM SAUCE

3 tablespoons Clarified Butter
  (page 146)
1 ⅓ cups raw mushroom
  stems, wiped clean and sliced
1 bay leaf
½ teaspoon Worcestershire
  sauce
2 tablespoons brandy
1 ⅓ cups whipping cream
Salt and white pepper to taste
1 ½ pounds veal loin, cut in
  medallions
2 tablespoons dry white wine
2 teaspoons minced fresh
  chives
Hot asparagus spears and new
  potatoes for accompaniment

In a skillet heat 1 ½ tablespoons of the butter, add
mushrooms and bay leaf and
cook over medium-high heat,
stirring, until mushrooms
darken a little. Add the Worcestershire sauce. Warm the
brandy, ignite, and pour over
the mushrooms, shaking pan
until flames are extinguished.
Add the cream and gently boil,
stirring, until cream has reduced and thickened. Strain
and discard mushrooms. Season with salt and pepper. Set
aside.

In a large skillet heat the remaining butter and when it
stops foaming, add meat.
Quickly sear and cook about 2
minutes on each side, or just
until cooked to desired doneness. Transfer to a warm plate.
Deglaze pan with wine. Add
the mushroom-infused cream
to the pan juices and heat
through. Stir in chives. Add
the medallions of veal to heat
through. Serve meat with
sauce under or over it. Accompany with hot cooked asparagus spears and new potatoes, if
desired. Makes 4 servings.

PRALINE ICE CREAM PIE

½ cup firmly packed brown
  sugar
½ cup whipping cream
2 tablespoons butter
1 cup chopped pecans
1 teaspoon vanilla extract
1 ½ quarts vanilla ice cream
9-inch baked Pastry Shell (page
  150)
3 egg whites
¼ teaspoon cream of tartar
⅓ cup sugar
Rum Sauce (following)

In a medium skillet heat brown
sugar, stirring, over medium-
low heat just until sugar melts,
about 10 to 12 minutes. Gradually blend in cream and cook 2
to 3 minutes longer, or until
smooth. Remove from heat and
stir in butter, pecans and vanilla. Cool.
    Let ice cream soften slightly
and quickly fold in praline mixture. Turn into pastry shell.

Cover and freeze. Just before
serving beat egg whites with
cream of tartar until soft peaks
form and gradually beat in the
sugar, beating until stiff peaks
form. Spread meringue over ice
cream, sealing to the edge.
Bake in a 475°F. oven for 4 to 5
minutes, or until lightly
browned. Serve immediately
with Rum Sauce. Makes 8
servings.

RUM SAUCE In a small saucepan
combine 2 beaten egg yolks, ½
teaspoon grated lemon peel,
¼ cup fresh lemon juice, ¼ cup
sugar and 4 tablespoons butter.
Cook and stir until thickened.
Stir in 3 tablespoons light rum.
Makes about 1 cup sauce.

A WINTER DINNER

Cream of Artichoke Soup with
Crushed Hazelnuts

Roast Glazed Fillet of Pork
with Gingered Orange Sauce

Wild Rice

Sautéed Sugar Snap Peas

Limestone Lettuce Salad

Apple Pithivier

CREAM OF ARTICHOKE SOUP WITH CRUSHED HAZELNUTS

4 large artichokes
⅓ cup hazelnuts
5 cups Chicken Stock (page
  147)
2 tablespoons cornstarch
  blended with 2 tablespoons
  cold water
⅔ cup whipping cream
Salt and white pepper to taste
Freshly grated nutmeg
2 tablespoons dry sherry

Remove leaves and stems from artichokes and scrape out the fuzzy center choke. Trim well, retaining only the bottoms. Poach artichoke bottoms in boiling salted water for 30 to 35 minutes or until very tender. Toast hazelnuts in a 325°F. oven for 10 minutes or until lightly browned. Rub off the skins and let cool. Grind finely in a food processor or blender. In a large saucepot place the artichoke bottoms, stock and ground hazelnuts. Bring to a boil, cover, and simmer 20 minutes. Puree until blended and blend in cornstarch paste. Return to the saucepan and cook, stirring, until thickened, about 2 minutes. Stir in cream, salt and pepper, nutmeg and sherry. Makes 6 servings.

ROAST GLAZED FILLET OF PORK WITH GINGERED ORANGE SAUCE

⅓ cup plus 2 tablespoons vegetable oil
¼ cup soy sauce
1 teaspoon coarsely ground black pepper
2 tablespoons dark rum
2 garlic cloves, crushed
1 tablespoon each diced carrot, celery and onion
1 teaspoon each chopped fresh thyme and rosemary or ¼ teaspoon each dried thyme and rosemary
⅛ teaspoon Worcestershire sauce
1 ½ teaspoons finely minced ginger root
½ bay leaf
2 pound boneless pork fillet
Gingered Orange Sauce (following)
Wild rice and sautéed sugar snap peas for accompaniment

For marinade, mix together in a bowl ⅓ cup of the oil, soy sauce, pepper, rum, garlic, carrot, celery, onion, thyme, rosemary, Worcestershire sauce, ginger root and bay leaf. Add pork fillet and let marinate 1 hour or longer, turning meat occasionally. Meanwhile, prepare Gingered Orange Sauce.

In a skillet brown pork fillet in remaining 2 tablespoons vegetable oil quickly on all sides. Place meat on a rack in a roasting pan and roast in a 450°F. oven for 15 to 18 minutes, or until temperature reaches 160°F. on a meat thermometer. Remove from oven and let sit 10 minutes. Slice meat on the diagonal. To serve, spoon a small amount of sauce on a platter or individual plates, arrange meat slices on top and spoon sauce over all. Accompany with wild rice and sautéed sugar snap peas, if desired. Makes 6 servings.

GINGERED ORANGE SAUCE Using a vegetable peeler, peel six strips of orange zest from an orange and place in a saucepan with ½ cup orange juice, ¼ cup sugar, 2 teaspoons finely diced ginger root, ⅛ teaspoon coarsely ground black pepper, ⅓ cup red wine vinegar and 2 teaspoons Grand Marnier. Bring to a boil and simmer uncovered for 30 minutes. Strain. In a separate saucepan combine 2 cups Demi-Glace (preferably made from duck wings, necks and gizzards or veal demi-glace) (page 148), 3 tablespoons currant jelly, 2 teaspoons tomato paste and 1 tablespoon rum. Simmer uncovered 30 minutes. Combine the two sauces and if necessary, reduce until sauce coats a spoon.

APPLE PITHIVIER

12 ounces Puff Pastry (page 149)
4 ounces almond paste (about ½ cup)
¼ pound unsalted butter
½ cup sugar
1 egg
½ cup all-purpose flour
½ teaspoon almond extract
1 large green apple (Granny Smith or Pippin)
Egg wash (1 egg yolk beaten with 1 tablespoon water)

Cut the puff pastry into one 4-ounce and one 8-ounce piece. Roll out the 4-ounce piece to make a 9-inch circle. Roll out the 8-ounce piece to make a 12-inch circle.

In a mixing bowl cream together the almond paste, butter and sugar until smooth. Add the egg, flour and almond extract and mix until smooth. Spread the almond mixture on the 9-inch pastry circle, leaving a 1-inch band around the outside edge. Peel, core and slice the apple. Fan the slices in a circle over the almond mixture. Brush the 1-inch band with egg wash and cover with the 12-inch circle. Seal the edges and mark a pattern on top with a sharp knife. Brush the top of the pastry with egg wash. Bake in a 400°F. oven for 25 minutes or until golden brown. Serve warm, cut into wedges. Makes 8 servings.

Naomi Schwartz
ST. ORRES
Gualala, California

The Russian fur trappers who settled this rugged, spectacular section of the Northern California coast would feel at home at the sight of the onion-shaped domes that top St. Orres, a fairy-tale inn and restaurant three-and-a-half hours north by car from San Francisco. Bursts of color from old-fashioned flower beds that border outside paths and from bouquets that fill the inner solarium add to St. Orres' wild beauty.

Stained glass windows, patchwork quilts and other handcrafted touches distinguish the inn's guest rooms and cottages; antiques fill its public rooms. Under one of the twin domes, the dining room soars three stories.

The kitchen, by contrast, is totally contemporary. Chef Naomi Schwartz, 35, is the talent behind the inspirational dinners and Sunday brunch, plus the lavish breakfast buffet board. She has headed the kitchen for the past three years, since graduating from the Culinary Institute of America. She first trained at West Valley College in Saratoga, California after her decision to make a career switch from teaching autistic children. Creativity with food is her decisive love.

Fresh fruits, vegetables and herbs are used with abundance in the courses. Blackberries and nectarines adorn a first course of smoked quail and wild rice in summer. Fresh dill scents a seafood sausage set afloat in a creamy beurre blanc. Escargots nestle in mushroom caps and French bucheron cheese is sealed in a flaky packet of filo partnered by crispy apple slices.

Main course specialties include breast of duckling laced with honey, lemon and green peppercorns accompanied by duck leg pâté and duck skin cracklings; breast of chicken stuffed with chicken mousse, chervil and chives; boneless quail with mushrooms and pancetta; seabass encased in seaweed and steamed and served with lemon butter

sauce; and medallions of veal with veal sweetbreads.

The ice cream maker supplies papaya, pineapple, kiwi and blueberry sorbets. Fruit tarts reflect the season. The whimsical dessert, Tulipe de Praline, is the most popular sweet and the house specialty. A caramelized walnut cookie, shaped like an oversize full-blown flower, holds coffee ice cream from the award-winning Mendocino Creamery with satiny chocolate sauce sealing all.

A SUMMER DINNER

Smoked Quail
with Napa Cabbage

Seafood Sausage in Filo with
Beurre Blanc

Wild Rice

Walnut Roulade
with Fresh Strawberries

SMOKED QUAIL WITH NAPA CABBAGE

¼ pound slab bacon, diced
½ cup balsamic vinegar
1 Napa cabbage, julienned
2 tablespoons chopped fresh
  parsley
4 smoked quail, boned
Cold cooked wild rice (about 2
  cups) for accompaniment

In a large skillet cook bacon until crispy; drain off the fat. Add vinegar and cabbage to the bacon and cook until cabbage is lightly braised, about 3 minutes. Add parsley. Spoon a mound of cabbage in the center of individual plates. Halve quail and arrange two halves on each cabbage bed. Accompany with wild rice. Makes 4 servings.

SEAFOOD SAUSAGE IN FILO WITH BEURRE BLANC

½ pound combination of raw
  prawns, scallops and salmon
Fish Stock (page 147)
1 ½ pounds sole
3 eggs
1 ¾ cups whipping cream
2 teaspoons salt
Pinch cayenne pepper
¼ teaspoon freshly ground
  black pepper
Pinch nutmeg
5 tablespoons snipped fresh
  dill or 2 teaspoons dried dill
Filo dough (about 6 sheets)
Melted butter
Buttered bread crumbs
Beurre Blanc (following)

Poach the prawns, scallops and salmon in fish stock just until barely tender, about 4 minutes; drain and chill. For sole mousse, in a food processor process the sole in on/off speeds with the eggs and cream alternating, ending with the cream. Blend in salt, cayenne, pepper, nutmeg and dill.

Cut the prawns, scallops and salmon into ¼-inch chunks.

Place in a bowl and stir in the sole mousse. Lightly oil a sheet of plastic wrap, turn out the seafood mixture onto it and shape into a log about 12 inches long and 3 inches thick. Roll up tightly and tie the ends.

Bring a large pot of water to a boil, add the plastic-wrapped sausage and let simmer very gently for about 25 minutes for a thin 3-inch roll or up to 45 minutes for a thicker roll. Remove, pat dry and chill 24 hours.

Remove plastic wrap. Lay out one sheet of filo (keep remainder covered with plastic wrap), brush with butter, and stack sheets of filo scattering the buttered bread crumbs between each layer. Place the sausage roll along one side and roll up, encasing it. Place on a buttered baking pan; brush top of roll with butter. Bake in a 375°F. oven for 20 minutes or until golden brown. Slice and serve warm with Beurre Blanc. Makes 8 servings.

BEURRE BLANC In a small saucepan reduce ½ cup dry white wine, 2 tablespoons chardonnay vinegar and 2 tablespoons minced shallots until liquid is reduced by half. Add ½ cup whipping cream and reduce by half. Add a small pinch of roux (a blend of 1 teaspoon butter and 1 teaspoon flour) and heat until open bubbles appear, about 30 seconds. Remove from heat and whisk in ¾ pound unsalted butter, one tablespoon at a time. Season with salt and freshly ground white pepper to taste. Makes about 2 cups sauce that holds well.

WALNUT ROULADE WITH FRESH STRAWBERRIES

6 eggs, separated
⅓ cup sugar
Pinch salt
¾ cup finely ground walnuts
Confectioners' sugar
1 pint whipping cream
2 tablespoons confectioners' sugar
2 teaspoons vanilla extract
3 cups sliced strawberries or kiwifruit
Whole strawberries or kiwi for garnish

In a large bowl beat egg yolks until light and lemon-colored and gradually beat in the sugar. In another bowl beat egg whites with salt until stiff peaks form. Mix the walnuts into the yolks and fold in the egg whites. Line a 9-by-13-inch pan with waxed paper and butter and flour the paper. Pour in the batter, spreading evenly. Bake in a 350°F. oven for 25 minutes or until the top springs back when touched lightly. Invert onto a towel dusted with confectioners' sugar, peel off the paper, and roll up lengthwise. Allow to cool.

Whip cream with the 2 tablespoons confectioners' sugar and vanilla, beating until stiff. Unroll cake, spread with half of the cream, cover with berries or kiwifruit and roll up. Place on a serving platter. Frost with remaining cream and garnish with berries. Makes 12 servings.

A WINTER DINNER

Goat Cheese in Filo

Loin of Lamb au Jus

Tulipe de Praline with Coffee Ice Cream and Hot Fudge Sauce

GOAT CHEESE IN FILO

8 ounces goat cheese
Filo (about 8 sheets)
4 ounces Clarified Butter (page 146)
2 large red-skinned apples for garnish

In a mixer or food processor blend cheese until soft and creamy. Lay out one sheet of filo (keep remainder covered with plastic wrap), brush with butter and cover with a second sheet of filo, and brush with butter. Cut into four strips. Spoon a mound of cheese at the end of each strip. Fold over in a triangle and continue folding in triangles until the end. Place on a buttered baking sheet. Brush tops of filo triangles with butter. Bake in a 375°F. oven for 15 minutes or until lightly browned. Serve hot, two triangles to a plate, garnished with thinly sliced apple flanking the triangles. Makes 4 servings.

LOIN OF LAMB AU JUS

1 saddle of lamb, boned (about
 4 ½ pounds before boning)
3 pounds fresh spinach,
 cooked, chopped and
 squeezed dry
4 garlic cloves, minced
Salt and freshly ground black
 pepper to taste
Lamb Sauce (following)
2 tablespoons tomato concasse
 (finely diced peeled tomato)

Have the butcher bone the saddle of lamb, removing all skin, yielding 2 loins and 2 tenderloins. Reserve bones for Lamb Sauce stock. Mix together the spinach, garlic and salt and pepper to taste. Place 1 loin on a board, cover with half the spinach and top with the tenderloin; tie neatly. Repeat with remaining meat and spinach.

Place on a rack in a roasting pan and roast in a 400°F. oven for about 15 minutes, turning to roast all sides, and cooking until meat is medium rare, about 145°F. on a meat thermometer. Remove from oven and let sit 15 minutes. Slice into ½ -inch scallops and arrange four on each plate with the tenderloin facing inward. Spoon over the Lamb Sauce and garnish with tomato concasse. Makes 6 servings.

LAMB SAUCE Have ready 1 quart Lamb Stock (page 147), made with lamb bones and part veal bones, if desired. Reduce lamb stock by half. Add 1 cup cabernet sauvignon wine or other dry red wine and reduce again by half. Makes about 1 ½ cups sauce.

TULIPE DE PRALINE

¼ pound unsalted butter
⅔ cup firmly packed brown
 sugar
2 tablespoons whipping cream
2 tablespoons all-purpose flour
1 cup finely chopped walnuts
Coffee ice cream
Hot Fudge Sauce (following)
Whipped cream for garnish
Mint sprigs for garnish

For tulip shells, in a saucepan combine the butter, brown sugar, cream and flour. Bring to a boil, stirring, and boil 1 minute. Remove from heat and stir in walnuts. Spoon about ¼ cup of batter onto a greased cookie sheet, spacing batter several inches apart. Bake in a 325°F. oven for 6 to 8 minutes, or until brown. Remove from oven; let cool 1 minute. Remove cookie with a spatula and lay over an inverted large custard cup, shaping it into a bowl. Repeat with remaining batter. Let cool. Store in a tightly closed container until ready to serve.

At serving time, fill each cookie shell with two scoops of ice cream. Spoon over the Hot Fudge Sauce and garnish with whipped cream and a mint sprig. Makes 8 servings.

HOT FUDGE SAUCE In a double boiler over hot water heat 4 ounces semisweet chocolate, ½ cup whipping cream and 1 tablespoon rum, stirring, until blended.

Marcel Desaulniers
THE TRELLIS
Williamsburg, Virginia

The Trellis is a beautiful, contemporary restaurant, with outdoor cafe, that invokes a California mood. It is located on the historic Duke of Gloucester Street in Williamsburg, Virginia. Two hundred fifty guests can be accommodated at one sitting.

The building is a 1936 Georgian revival that for forty-three years was a drugstore. The interior was completely gutted when it was transformed into a restaurant five years ago. Vines of Delaware grapes cover the entrance. The rooms are paneled in heart pine with similarly-colored tiles on the floor. Greenery, a Venetian glass chandelier, antique wine prints, French harvest baskets and vineyard tools provide accents.

Here executive chef and co-owner Marcel Desaulniers, 37, sets forth imaginative seasonal fare. "Fresh is our most important criterion," Desaulniers states.

The changing menu reflects an American regional tone. Offerings encompass red snapper with sunchokes and jalapeño chilies; grilled chicken breast with pears, cider, cream and wild mushroom fettuccine; grilled medallions of pork with cranberries and sweet potato fettuccine.

Pastries include cheesecakes, dacquoise and a wealth of ice creams, from several chocolate flavors to tequila grapefruit, boysenberry or pineapple-coconut sorbet.

Desaulniers grew up in Rhode Island in a French Canadian community. He spoke only French until first grade. During high school he worked in a restaurant, the Tower, in Uxbridge, Massachusetts, serving as busboy, dishwasher, waiter and cook. The owner encouraged him to attend the Culinary Institute of America and signed the loan Desaulniers needed to pay his tuition. He graduated in 1965.

Since 1970 he has been in Williamsburg where he began by working for the Colonial Williamsburg Foundation catering parties for visiting international dignitaries.

A SUMMER DINNER

Chilled English Stilton Soup

Grilled Marinated
Breast of Chicken
with Scallions, Radishes
and Lime

Sautéed Golden and Green
Zucchini

Pineapple-Coconut Sorbet

CHILLED ENGLISH STILTON SOUP

2 teaspoons vegetable oil
2 inner stalks celery, diced
1 small onion, diced
1 leek, diced (white part only)
3 cups Chicken Stock (page 147)
1 tablespoon cornstarch blended with 2 tablespoons cold water
3 ounces grated Monterey jack cheese
1 cup half-and-half
2 Bartlett or Anjou pears, cored and diced for garnish
3 ounces Stilton cheese, diced for garnish
Small rounds Puff Pastry for garnish (page 149)

In a heavy saucepot heat oil and sauté celery, onion and leek until transparent, about 5 minutes. Add stock and bring to a boil. Cover and simmer 15 minutes. Puree in a food processor or blender. Return to the saucepot, bring to a boil and stir in the cornstarch paste. Cook, stirring, until thickened, about 2 minutes. Stir in the grated Monterey jack cheese and set on ice to cool. Stir in half-and-half and chill.

At serving time ladle into bowls and garnish with diced pears and Stilton cheese. Top with puff pastry, if desired. Makes 4 servings.

GRILLED MARINATED BREAST OF CHICKEN WITH SCALLIONS, RADISHES AND LIME

4 chicken breast halves, boned and skinned
Salt
3 tablespoons fresh lemon juice
1 1/2 teaspoons whole coriander
1 1/2 teaspoons whole cumin
2 tablespoons minced ginger root
1 1/2 teaspoons minced garlic
1/4 teaspoon cayenne pepper
1 pint plain yogurt
Julienned radishes and green onions for garnish
2 limes, quartered for garnish

Sprinkle chicken breasts lightly with salt and lemon juice and let stand 30 minutes. Place the coriander and cumin in a small pie pan and bake in a 350°F. oven for 5 minutes or until lightly toasted. Let cool. Pulverize in a mortar with pestle. Turn into a bowl and mix in ginger root, garlic, pepper and yogurt. Turn chicken breasts in the yogurt mixture and let marinate, refrigerated, for 24 hours. To serve, grill chicken over medium-hot coals, or broil, turning to cook both sides, basting occasionally with the marinade. Cover a serving platter or individual plates with the radish julienne. Top with chicken and garnish with green onions and limes. Makes 4 servings.

PINEAPPLE-COCONUT SORBET

1 ½ cups water
1 cup sugar
1 can (15 ounces) cream of coconut
1 cup grated coconut
1 large pineapple, peeled, halved, cored and pureed
1 tablespoon fresh lemon juice

In a saucepan bring water and sugar to a boil and let simmer 5 minutes. Cool. Stir in the cream of coconut, coconut, pineapple puree and lemon juice. Chill thoroughly. Churn in an ice cream freezer following manufacturer's instructions until frozen. Makes about 2 quarts.

A WINTER DINNER

Chesapeake Oysters and Shiitake Mushrooms in Brioche

Loin Lamb Chops with Peppers and Mint

Pilaf

Petite Green Beans with Tarragon

Romaine Salad with Apple and Oregon Tillamook Cheese

The Trellis Chocolate Mousse Cake

CHESAPEAKE OYSTERS AND SHIITAKE MUSHROOMS IN BRIOCHE

1 pint whipping cream
4 ounces shiitake mushrooms, thinly sliced
2 tablespoons dry white wine
1 teaspoon chopped shallots
4 to 6 small Brioche (page 149) or frozen brioche, heated
1 pint Chesapeake oysters
Salt and freshly ground black pepper to taste
Watercress for garnish

In a heavy saucepan, bring cream to a boil, then simmer until reduced by half. In another pan place mushrooms, wine and shallots and let simmer 10 minutes.

Heat brioche in a 350°F. oven for 10 minutes, or until hot through. Split open and hollow out insides slightly. Add oysters to the shiitake mushrooms and cook only until oysters begin to curl, about 2 minutes. Add the reduced cream to the oysters and mushrooms and season with salt and pepper. To serve, arrange brioche on plates and spoon the hot oyster mixture equally into the warm brioche. Place tops on brioche and garnish with watercress. Makes 4 to 6 servings.

LOIN LAMB CHOPS WITH PEPPERS AND MINT

1 large onion, sliced
4 tablespoons butter
1 green pepper, seeded and sliced
1 sweet red pepper, seeded and sliced
8 ounces mushrooms, sliced
1 tablespoon chopped fresh mint
Salt and freshly ground black pepper to taste
12 loin lamb chops (2 chops per person)
Mint Butter (following)
Mint sprigs for garnish
Enoki mushrooms for garnish*

In a large skillet sauté onion in butter for 5 minutes or until translucent. Add peppers, mushrooms and mint and sauté 3 to 4 minutes longer, stirring. Remove from heat and season with salt and pepper. Reserve, keeping warm.

Season lamb chops with salt and pepper. Grill over a charcoal and wood fire basting with Mint Butter and turning to brown both sides, cooking to desired doneness, about 3 minutes on a side for medium rare.

To serve, place mushroom-and-pepper mixture on plates, set grilled chops on top and garnish each plate with sprigs of fresh mint and enoki mushrooms. Makes 6 servings.

MINT BUTTER Mix together 3 tablespoons softened butter, 2 minced garlic cloves, and 2 teaspoons chopped fresh mint.

Available at Oriental or specialty produce markets.

THE TRELLIS CHOCOLATE MOUSSE CAKE

¼ pound semisweet chocolate
¼ pound unsalted butter, cut in cubes
4 egg yolks
½ cup sugar
3 egg whites
Chocolate Mousse Frosting (following)
1 tablespoon cocoa powder
1 teaspoon confectioners' sugar

In the top of a double boiler heat chocolate and butter over hot water until melted, stirring to blend. Remove from heat. Beat egg yolks until thick and light in color and gradually beat in sugar, beating well. Stir in chocolate mixture.

Beat egg whites until stiff, but not dry. Add one-third of the whites to the chocolate mixture and mix in. Fold in the remaining whites. Lightly butter the bottom and sides of an 8- or 9-inch springform pan. Pour in batter. Bake in a 325°F. oven for 30 minutes for the 9-inch pan or 40 minutes for the 8-inch pan. Let cool on a rack. Then turn out onto a plate and let stand until thoroughly cooled. Frost top and sides with Chocolate Mousse Frosting. Dust with cocoa through a sieve and top with confectioners' sugar dusted through a sieve. Chill until firm. Makes 8 to 10 servings.

CHOCOLATE MOUSSE FROSTING In a double boiler heat ¼ pound unsweetened chocolate and ¼ pound butter, cut in cubes, over hot water, stirring until blended. Beat 4 egg yolks until thick and light in color and gradually beat in ½ cup sugar, beating well. Stir in chocolate mixture. Beat 3 egg whites until stiff, but not dry, and fold in.

James Moore
ZUNI CAFE
San Francisco, California

East meets West in the wide-open kitchen of the Zuni Cafe. There chef James Moore, 43, borrows from the cuisines of the world to put his personal stamp on West Coast regional American cooking.

Whitewashed walls, brightly colored serapi seat cushions, small, square stone tables and bouquets of lilies and eucalyptus lend a southwestern air to the high-ceilinged, two-story restaurant.

The blackboard lists daily changing specialties like warm spinach salad with sweetbreads and pecans; carpaccio with Parmesan; fettuccine with spinach and yellow peppers; frittata-style omelet with chorizo sausage, queso and salsa fresca; grilled chicken and pork sausage with polenta and black beans; and leg of lamb with cumin wine marinade. Winning desserts include ginger crème caramel, fresh poached fruit compote, ground pecan cake on maple crème anglaise and homemade ices and ice creams.

Moore's love of cooking comes from his Czech-Polish grandmother with whom he often cooked as a boy. About six years ago he left a career in public relations to enter the California Culinary Academy in San Francisco as a student and stayed on as a chef-instructor. He continues to teach on occasion throughout the country, sharing "food that people can do with ease." Spare time finds him browsing among his collection of thousands of cookbooks, or dining out, preferably in New York City. He has been chef at the Zuni Cafe for three years.

AN ALL-SEASONS MENU

Sweet Potato Soup with Jalapeños and Lime Cream

Grilled Chicken and Assorted Peppers

Seasonal Fruit Compote

SWEET POTATO SOUP WITH JALAPENOS AND LIME CREAM

3 to 4 medium sweet potatoes
  or yams
1 cup diced onions
2 tablespoons unsalted butter
4 cups Chicken Stock (page
  147)
1 to 2 jalapeño peppers, seeded
  and finely diced
Salt to taste
Lime Cream (following)
Lime zest for garnish

Cook sweet potatoes whole, unpeeled, in boiling salted water until tender, about 1 hour. Drain, cool and peel. In a skillet sauté onions in butter.

In a food processor or blender puree the potatoes, onions and part of the stock. Return to a saucepan with remaining stock. Add jalapeño peppers and salt. Cover and simmer for 30 minutes. Ladle into soup bowls. Drizzle a spoonful of Lime Cream in a circular pattern on each serving and swirl with a spoon. Garnish each with 2 or 3 strips of lime zest. Makes 4 servings.

LIME CREAM Stir the grated peel and juice of 1 lime into ½ cup sour cream, adding just enough juice to make a pourable consistency.

GRILLED CHICKEN AND ASSORTED PEPPERS

⅓ cup olive oil
¼ cup fresh lemon juice or
  fresh grapefruit juice
3 tablespoons washed
  fermented black beans*
1 bunch cilantro, chopped
2 chickens (about 1 ¾ pounds
  each), split down backbone
6 long sweet red peppers or red
  bell peppers
Lemon-Oil Baste (1 tablespoon
  lemon juice blended with 2
  tablespoons olive oil)
Orange Pepper Sauce
  (following)
Cilantro sprigs for garnish
Orange Zest (following)

Mix together the olive oil, lemon juice, black beans and chopped cilantro. Add chicken, opened to lay flat, and let marinate, refrigerated, 1 day.

Split peppers lengthwise, remove seeds. Brush with Lemon-Oil Baste. Grill peppers over medium-hot coals. Add chicken and grill, turning peppers and chicken, until cooked through, about 15 minutes.

Arrange chicken on plates and spoon over the Orange Pepper Sauce. Garnish with cilantro sprigs and Orange Zest. Makes 2 servings.

ORANGE PEPPER SAUCE In a skillet place 3 tablespoons washed fermented black beans, 1 tablespoon chopped jalapeño pepper, ½ cup chopped cilantro, ½ teaspoon chopped ginger root, 2 minced garlic cloves, and 1 cup Chicken Stock (page 147). Cook down until sauce coats a spoon. In a separate pan reduce 1 cup fresh orange juice until syrupy. Combine stock mixture and orange juice and season with salt and freshly ground black pepper to taste. Whisk in 1 tablespoon butter. Add a few drops fresh lemon juice.

ORANGE ZEST With a vegetable peeler peel the strips from 1 orange; julienne. Blanch in hot water for 5 minutes. Drain.

Available at Oriental markets.

SEASONAL FRUIT COMPOTE

1 strip lime zest
2 cups dry red or white wine
⅔ cup honey (preferably an herbal honey to match the herb used)
1 ½ tablespoons lime juice
Herbs: 6 sprigs thyme, 2 bay leaves or 8 white peppercorns
6 pieces new crop dried fruits: white or black figs, pitted prunes, apricot halves or nectarines
6 pears: Bosc, Bartlett or Anjou
Lightly whipped cream for garnish
Preserved sliced kumquats for garnish (optional)

Use a vegetable peeler to strip off the lime zest. Place in a saucepan with the wine, honey, lime juice and herbs. Bring to a simmer, add dried fruit and poach until just tender, about 6 to 8 minutes. With a slotted spoon, remove fruit to a colander placed over a bowl to let juices drain; reserve honey syrup.

Peel, core and cut pears into ½ -inch-thick wedges. In a skillet simmer pears in the honey syrup until just tender, about 10 to 15 minutes. Add pears to the colander and let drain. Strain and boil down the poaching liquid to a light syrup, adding any juices from the drained fruit. Add fruits to the syrup and chill overnight. Serve at room temperature with lightly whipped cream and preserved sliced kumquats, if desired. Makes 6 servings.

A WINTER MENU

Grilled Cumin Chicken and Orange Salad

Pasta with Oysters, Spicy Sausage and Watercress

Chocolate Cake with Almonds

GRILLED CUMIN CHICKEN AND ORANGE SALAD

4 chicken breast halves, boned
2 tablespoons cumin seeds
2 cups plain yogurt
Salt and freshly ground black
  pepper to taste
1 tablespoon mint leaves or
  cilantro, chopped
4 to 5 tablespoons fresh orange
  juice
¼ cup olive oil
Salad greens: butter lettuce,
  baby spinach, curly endive,
  red leaf lettuce
2 oranges, peeled and
  sectioned
Freshly ground pepper
Mint or cilantro sprigs for
  garnish

Pound chicken breasts lightly to make evenly thick. Toast cumin seeds in a skillet over medium heat, tossing constantly until lightly browned. Turn out onto a plate and let cool. Pulverize in a mortar with pestle. Rub chicken lightly with about 2 teaspoons cumin.

For marinade, combine 1 ¼ cups yogurt with 2 teaspoons cumin, salt and pepper and 1 tablespoon chopped mint leaves. Marinate the chicken, refrigerated, for 6 hours or longer.

Let warm to room temperature for 1 hour before grilling. Brush off excess marinade and grill chicken 4 to 5 minutes per side or until tender, basting with a mixture of 2 tablespoons orange juice and olive oil, and cooking just until barely tender. Cool to room temperature. Remove skin. With hands shred chicken into bite-sized pieces.

For dressing, combine remaining ¾ cup yogurt with 2 teaspoons ground cumin, salt and pepper to taste and about 2 to 3 tablespoons orange juice, or enough to make a pourable consistency.

To serve, tear crisped greens into generous bite-sized pieces and toss with enough dressing to coat lightly. Mound on individual plates. Nestle chicken and orange sections on and between the leaves. Sprinkle with freshly ground black pepper and garnish each with a sprig of mint or cilantro. Makes 4 servings.

PASTA WITH OYSTERS, SPICY SAUSAGE AND WATERCRESS

2 lengths of spicy sausage (6
  inches each), such as hot
  Italian sausage or andouille
  (not chorizo)
2 ½ cups oysters
2 tablespoons chopped shallots
1 ½ teaspoons butter
1 tablespoon chopped fresh
  parsley
1 ½ cups whipping cream
Juice of ½ lemon
1 bunch watercress
12 ounces fresh egg fettuccine
Lemon wedges for garnish

Prick casings on sausages. Blanch for 5 minutes, then grill or pan fry until cooked through.

Remove 4 oysters and poach or grill for garnish. In a food processor or blender, puree the remaining oysters along with the oyster liquor. In a medium sauté pan sauté shallots in butter. Add oyster puree, shallots, parsley and cream. Simmer gently to reduce by 10 percent and thicken slightly. Skim froth. Add lemon juice.

Reserve 4 sprigs watercress for garnish; pick leaves from rest of watercress and chop. Cook pasta in boiling salted water until just tender; drain and toss with the oyster cream sauce. Toss in the chopped watercress. Turn out on a platter or plates and crumble sausage over the top. Garnish with poached oysters, sprigs of watercress and lemon wedges. Makes 4 servings.

CHOCOLATE CAKE WITH ALMONDS

9 ounces semisweet chocolate, chopped
5 ounces unsalted butter, softened
1 tablespoon brandy
4 eggs, separated
½ cup plus 5 tablespoons sugar
⅛ teaspoon cream of tartar
5 tablespoons all-purpose flour
½ cup ground blanched almonds
Lightly whipped cream for garnish

In a double boiler melt chocolate over hot water. Stir in butter in bits with brandy, stirring until blended. Cool. In a mixing bowl beat egg yolks at high speed for 2 minutes. Continue beating and gradually add ½ cup of the sugar, beating until it forms a ribbon.

Beat the egg whites at very low speed for 3 to 4 minutes; beat at medium speed 1 minute; then beat at high speed, add the cream of tartar, and gradually add the 5 tablespoons sugar, beating until soft peaks form.

Stir chocolate into the yolk mixture. Mix together the flour and nuts and stir into the yolks. Stir one-third of the whites into the yolks and barely fold in the remaining whites, letting small swirls of whites remain. Line the bottom of a buttered 8-inch springform pan with waxed paper. Butter and flour the paper and the pan sides. Pour in the batter and tap down to remove air bubbles. Bake in a 350°F. oven for 40 minutes or until firm to touch and the top is puffed and cracked. Cool in the pan and unmold. Serve at room temperature with lightly whipped cream. Makes 8 to 10 servings.

BASIC RECIPES

CLARIFIED BUTTER

Slowly melt butter in a saucepan over moderate heat. Remove from heat and skim off scum that rises to the surface. Let stand to allow milk solids to settle. Pour clear butter into a container and discard milk. Clarified butter is also known as drawn butter.

CREME ANGLAISE

3 egg yolks
2 tablespoons sugar
1 cup hot milk
1 teaspoon vanilla extract or 1 teaspoon grated lemon peel

Beat egg yolks with sugar until light in color. Turn into a double boiler and stir in 1 cup hot milk. Cook over hot water, stirring, until custard coats a spoon. Remove from heat and stir in vanilla extract or grated lemon peel. Cool and refrigerate. Makes 1 ½ cups sauce.

CREME FRAICHE

Combine 1 cup whipping cream and ½ cup sour cream in a saucepan. Stir to blend and heat just to 80°F. Remove from heat, cover and let stand at room temperature until very thick, about 12 hours or overnight. Refrigerate. Makes about 1 ½ cups.

BEURRE BLANC

3 tablespoons white wine vinegar
2 shallots, very finely chopped, or green onions (white part only), very finely chopped
3 tablespoons dry white wine
½ pound butter, cut in small pieces
Salt and white pepper to taste

In a saucepan boil vinegar and shallots until liquid is reduced to 1 tablespoon. Add wine and boil until reduced to 2 tablespoons. Over very low heat, gradually whisk in butter, one tablespoon at a time, to obtain an emulsion. Remove from heat, if necessary, while incorporating the butter to maintain the right temperature. Makes about 1 cup sauce.

HOLLANDAISE SAUCE

3 egg yolks
2 tablespoons fresh lemon juice
½ teaspoon grated lemon peel
¼ teaspoon salt
Approximately ¼ pound butter

Rinse out blender container with very hot water and drain. In the container place the egg yolks, lemon juice, lemon peel and salt and blend a few seconds. Melt butter until bubbly. With blender motor running, gradually pour in butter in a slow, steady stream, omitting the milky residue at the bottom of the butter pan and blending just until smooth. Turn sauce into a double boiler and heat gently over hot water, or heat in a small saucepan. Makes about 1 cup.

BEEF STOCK

3 to 4 pounds raw, meaty beef
  bones
2 onions, chopped
1 carrot, peeled and chopped
1 stalk celery, chopped
Few celery leaves
Bouquet garni (3 sprigs parsley,
  1 bay leaf and 2 sprigs thyme,
  tied in a cheesecloth bag)
2 cloves garlic
Water
2 teaspoons salt or to taste

Place bones in a roasting pan
and roast in a 450°F. oven for 20
to 30 minutes, or until
browned. Transfer to a soup
kettle. Add onions, carrot, celery, celery leaves, bouquet
garni tied in the cheesecloth
bag and garlic. Pour in water to
cover and add salt. Simmer
partially covered for 3 to 4
hours, skimming off foam, and
adding more water if necessary. Strain, skim the fat and
refrigerate or freeze until
needed. Makes about 2 quarts.

VEAL STOCK Substitute veal
bones for the beef bones and
prepare as above.

LAMB STOCK Substitute lamb
bones for the beef bones and
prepare as above.

DUCK STOCK Substitute duck
bones for the beef bones and
prepare as above. If desired,
extend the duck bones with
veal bones.

CHICKEN STOCK

3 to 4 pounds chicken necks
  and wings
2 quarts water
2 teaspoons salt
1 onion, quartered
1 stalk celery, sliced
1 carrot, peeled and halved

In a large soup pot place the
chicken necks and wings,
water, salt, onion, celery and
carrot. Cover and simer 1 ½

hours. Remove chicken parts,
strain stock and chill. Skim fat
when cool. Makes about 1 ½
quarts stock.

FISH STOCK

1 ½ to 2 pounds fish bones and
  heads
1 ½ quarts water
2 cups dry white wine or dry
  vermouth
1 tablespoon chopped fresh
  thyme or ¾ teaspoon dried
  thyme
2 onions, peeled and stuck
  with 2 whole cloves
2 carrots, diced
2 garlic cloves
1 bay leaf
Salt to taste
4 peppercorns

In a large soup pot simmer fish
bones and heads in water for
30 minutes. Strain through a
fine sieve. Return stock to pot
and add wine, thyme, onions,
carrots, garlic, bay leaf, salt
and peppercorns. Bring to a
boil and simmer 20 minutes.
Strain. Makes about 1 ¾
quarts.

DEMI-GLACE

This sauce begins with a long-simmered brown meat sauce: beef, veal or lamb stock simmered and skimmed for several hours until it is reduced to a thick sauce that coats the back of a spoon. Start with a basic Beef Stock, Veal Stock, Lamb Stock, or Duck Stock but double or triple the recipe depending on quantity desired, as 2 quarts of beef stock will reduce down to about ⅓ to ½ cup of Demi-Glace. Allow at least 12 hours to achieve this process.

GLACE DE VIANDE

This meat glaze is prepared from a demi-glace boiled and reduced to a syrup that becomes a hard jelly when it is cold.

POACHED SWEETBREADS

Wash sweetbreads in cold water, then place in a bowl and soak in several changes of cold water for 1 ½ to 2 hours. Pull off the filaments which enclose them, then soak again for 1 ½ to 2 hours in several changes of cold water containing 1 tablespoon vinegar per quart of water. Peel off any more filament that comes off readily.

In a large saucepan place sweetbreads and cover by 2 inches with cold water; add 1 teaspoon salt and 1 tablespoon lemon juice or white wine vinegar per quart of water. Bring to a simmer and cook, uncovered, for 15 minutes. Drain and plunge into cold water for 5 minutes. Drain again.

PASTA DOUGH

3 cups all-purpose flour
1 teaspoon salt
¼ cup water
3 tablespoons safflower or olive
  oil
3 eggs

Place flour and salt in a mixing bowl and make a well in the center. Add water, oil and eggs. With finger tips or a fork, mix until flour is blended in and shape into a ball. Or if desired, place all ingredients in the bowl of a heavy duty electric mixer and mix until it forms a ball. Knead on a lightly floured board until dough is smooth and elastic, about 10 minutes. Cover with plastic wrap and let rest 10 minutes before rolling out.

For fettuccine or tagliarini noodles, divide dough into four portions. Feed through a pasta machine and cut as desired.

For ravioli dough, divide dough into three portions and feed through a pasta machine making long strips.

BRIOCHE

1 package active dry yeast
⅓ cup lukewarm water
¾ cup butter
2 tablespoons sugar
1 teaspoon salt
4 eggs
3 ¼ cups all-purpose flour
  (approximately)
1 egg white, lightly beaten

Sprinkle yeast into warm water and stir until dissolved. Beat butter until creamy, then beat in sugar, salt, and eggs, beating well after each addition. Add 1 cup flour and beat until smooth. Stir in yeast mixture. Gradually add remaining flour, beating well, adding enough to make a soft dough. Turn out on a floured board and knead until smooth and satiny. Place in a greased bowl, butter top of dough lightly, cover with a clean kitchen towel, and let rise in a warm place until doubled in size. Punch down and refrigerate at least 6 hours or up to 24 hours.

Turn out onto a floured board and knead lightly. Divide dough into about a dozen pieces for individual brioches. Pinch off one-fourth of each piece of dough and shape both large and small pieces into balls. Place a large ball in each buttered 3-inch brioche pan. Make a cross on top of each, shape the smaller ball into a teardrop and insert in the cross. Cover with a towel and let rise until almost tripled or pans are almost full. Brush tops with lightly beaten egg white. Bake in a 425°F. oven for 20 minutes or until golden brown. Makes about 1 dozen brioche.

PUFF PASTRY

Commercially available frozen puff pastry shells and puff pastry sheets are a fine shortcut to making pastry crescents, shells, diamonds or rectangles. A 10-ounce package of puff pastry shells yields 6 shells when baked. A 17-ounce package of puff pastry sheets provides about 10 to 12 diamonds or rectangles or 2 dozen crescents.

Bake the puff pastry shells according to package directions. To shape the puff pastry sheets into crescents, diamonds or rectangles, let pastry thaw. Place on a board and cut out with a knife or a cutter. Place on a baking sheet and refrigerate to firm up dough. Bake in a 425°F. oven allowing 10 minutes for the crescents and 15 to 20 minutes for the diamonds or rectangles.

PUFF PASTRY

⅔ cup unsalted butter
1 ⅓ cups all-purpose flour
⅔ cup cake flour
1 teaspoon salt
Approximately ½ cup ice water

Place butter on a sheet of waxed paper and lightly flour it. Cover with a sheet of waxed paper and flatten with a rolling pin. Remove top sheet of paper and fold butter in half, replace paper and continue folding and rolling until butter is pliable but not sticky. Shape into a 6-inch square and flour it. Mix together the all-purpose flour, cake flour, salt and enough ice water to form coarse crumbs. Press into a ball. Wrap in plastic wrap and refrigerate 15 minutes.

Roll dough to a 12-inch square slightly thicker in the center than at the sides. Place butter in center and fold dough like an envelope. Place seam down and flatten slightly. Roll into a rectangle about 8 inches wide and 18 inches long. Fold like a letter; press seams with rolling pin to seal and give it a turn. Again roll into a large rectangle and fold in thirds for a second turn.

Wrap in plastic wrap and refrigerate 15 minutes. Repeat rolling process, giving dough 6 turns altogether, and letting it rest in the refrigerator several hours after the fourth turn. Refrigerate 1 hour before shaping. It may be refrigerated up to 3 days before using. Makes approximately 1 pound.

TART SHELL

1 cup all-purpose flour
¼ pound butter
2 tablespoons confectioners'
  sugar

Place in a mixing bowl the flour, butter and sugar. Mix with an electric mixer until particles are crumbly. Pat into the bottom and sides of a 9- or 10-inch flan pan or 9-inch pie pan. Refrigerate for 30 minutes to firm up or freeze for 10 minutes. Bake in a 425°F. oven for 7 to 8 minutes to partially bake the shell, or bake 10 minutes or until lightly browned to bake completely. Makes a 9- or 10-inch pastry shell.

INDEX

DESSERTS

ENTREES

BIOGRAPHICAL NOTES

Lou Pappas' love for native American foods goes back to a childhood in the verdant Willamette Valley of Oregon. Here, everyday pleasures included picking huckleberries and wild blackberries, grilling salmon Indian style, savoring fresh Dungeness crab and churning homemade ice cream. After graduating from Oregon State University in home economics with a minor in journalism, she moved to California. Her zeal for fresh ingredients was enhanced by clamming and musseling along the coast and the joys of freshly picked fruits, vegetables and herbs from her garden. Lou's culinary knowledge and skills led to a job as food consultant for *Sunset* magazine and eventually to her present position as food editor of the *Peninsula Times Tribune* in Palo Alto, California, plus the publication of numerous articles in magazines such as *Gourmet* and *Cuisine*. She is also the author of fifteen cookbooks, most of which drew upon her extensive travels to Europe for their ethnic themes; she has made over a dozen trips in recent years to collect recipes. Now she writes about the subject dearest to her heart: creative American cookery based upon the season's bounty.